Meditation from the Heart of Judaism

MEDITATION
FROM THE HEART
OF JUDAISM

**Today's Teachers Share
Their Practices, Techniques, and Faith**

Edited by Avram Davis

Jewish Lights Publishing
Woodstock, Vermont

Meditation from the Heart of Judaism:
Today's Teachers Share Their Practices, Techniques, and Faith

1999 First Quality Paperback Edition

Library of Congress Cataloging-in-Publication Data
Meditation from the heart of Judaism : today's teachers share their
practices, techniques, and faith / edited by Avram Davis.
p.   cm.
ISBN 1-58023-049-0 (pbk)
ISBN 1-879045-77-X (hc)
1. Meditation—Judaism. 2. Spiritual life—Judaism. I. Davis, Avram.
BM723.M43 1997
296.7'2—dc21   97–35827
CIP
r97

10 9 8 7 6 5 4 3 2 1

Manufactured in the United States of America
Book and jacket designed by Glenn Suokko

For People of All Faiths, All Backgrounds
Published by Jewish Lights Publishing
A Division of LongHill Partners, Inc.
Sunset Farm Offices, Route 4, P.O. Box 237
Woodstock, Vermont 05091
Tel: (802) 457-4000 Fax: (802) 457-4004

www.jewishlights.com

To my daughters
Aliyah and Shaendl

and my students
that they should always
grow in Torah

Contents

Introduction:
The Heart of Jewish Meditation

AVRAM DAVIS

I believe the current revival of Jewish meditation is one of the best opportunities for the spiritual survival of the Jewish people. Disseminating the techniques of meditation and studying them, plus the development of *midot* (personal, spiritual qualities) that underpin meditation, are the next flowering of Torah.

Engaging in meditation, which entails transformation of Self, is a preeminent commandment of the Torah tradition. As the sixteenth-century Kabbalist Moses Cordovero wrote, pursuing meditation "constitutes [the reason for] existence in the world, its life-force and its nourishment...because of this science the world will receive great emanation."[1]

Meditation has been an integral part of Jewish spiritual practice for at least three millennia, but it was always reserved for an elite group rather than being a tool designed for ordinary people and used by ordinary people. For "ordinary" Jews, personal transformation came from such practices as rigid adherence to ritual *mitzvot* or from sacrifice, which entailed giving up something precious. But deep, contemplative work was left to a small group of very developed teachers, most of whom are known to us as prophets or sages of the Talmud, such as Hillel, Akiva, and Bar Yohai. This specialized lineage continued, sometimes growing larger, sometimes smaller, but essentially staying the same in terms of general accessibility. While these sages themselves were accessible to the people, the mystical and meditative wisdom they possessed was kept confined to their own circles.

BRINGING MEDITATION
TO THE PEOPLE

Though there have been numerous attempts over the last two millennia to "democratize" the meditative tradition and make it more available to the masses, these efforts have not been especially successful, and the tradition has remained in the hands of an elite. Yet, we are now experiencing a historic moment of expansion and transition. There is an expansion of the role of meditation within the Jewish tradition and a transition of meditation from a practice cultivated by only a very few to a mass movement. As meditation moves outward from a small core of people, it is becoming accessible to tens of thousands of people. This is occurring just as the need for meditation has been growing ever more acute, especially over the last decade. As we leave the post-Holocaust period, the horrors of those years are being healed by new tools of personal and group development.

The last ten years has also seen a rapid acceleration of the ills of modernity, such as expanding workloads, increased anonymity in the workplace and the private sphere, and a general loss of personal safety. Coupled with this, or perhaps partly because of this, we are entering a period in which people are very aware of what is missing from their lives, and they hunger for the Divine. While the majority of Americans are not theologically sophisticated, they are profoundly sophisticated about professional development, sexual matters, interpersonal dynamics, and psychology. This has translated into a demand for tools of personal transformation that, while not necessarily theologically complex, have great potential to help a person spiritually and psychologically and give them direct access to the Divine.

Some of these benefits are quite subtle; some are profoundly direct. Meeting the need for this profound interest in meditation is a handful of teachers trained in Jewish meditation.

Two schools in the United States, in fact, are training meditation teachers: Chochmat HaLev in Berkeley and Metivta in Los Angeles. However, despite the burgeoning interest, there are some misconceptions regarding Jewish meditation.

WHAT MAKES MEDITATION "JEWISH"

People often equate meditation with a trancelike state or with simple relaxation. Trance and relaxation are splendid conditions, but generally speaking, Jewish meditation is not so interested in inducing these alone. Meditation will indeed often produce a relaxed state or lowered blood pressure, but these are not the central reasons for meditation, since meditation is neither a drug nor hypnosis. Instead, meditation is meant to transform us from a state of ignorance to a state of wisdom, from a state of bondage (be it psychological or personal) to a state of being free. Because Judaism does not derive from a monastic tradition, it demands participation in the world.

All the teachers in this book subscribe to the notion that meditation is transformative, that it can bring us to a greater state of joy and inner freedom. Even when they engage in specialized concentration, these teachers present strategies to annihilate ego. This is an ultimate desire of the meditative path, for herein lies the infinite bliss of God. Issachar Baer, an eighteenth-century Hasidic leader taught, "The essence of serving

God...[is] to understand that...you are simply a channel for the divine attributes...[and that] you have no independent self."[2]

Some of the teachers in this book teach that proper meditation technique resides in our need to attach ourselves to the words or the visualizations we use. By doing this, ego is transferred or surrendered to the object being meditated upon. Through doing this again and again, practitioners realize that their own personality and ego are infinitely changeable and that there is ultimately nothing except the Infinite One. When this realization occurs, true *chochmat*, or wisdom, begins to dawn. As this realization deepens, *mochin gadlut,* literally "great mind," which can also be interpreted as enlightenment, becomes the dominant state.

THE DIRECT EXPERIENCE OF DIVINITY AND PERSONAL CHANGE

A common misunderstanding that arises concerning meditation, which the writers in this book work hard to dispel, is that it quickly dissipates our problems—usually encouraging the meditator to experience bliss or very "high" thoughts. But meditation is potentially quite boring. The changes within us that it generates can be very deep, but they do not necessarily occur quickly. For change to happen, even change for the good, often we must go through periods of great introspection, and this can be painful. Though some kabbalistic visualizations and formulations can be very complicated, most *chesed* (loving-kindness) and *ayin* (nothingness) techniques of meditation discussed in this book are very simple and direct. Ultimately, all of them are meant to bring us to a direct experience of ourselves and of God. These two things are not really separate, and meditation is designed to bring them together naturally.

All the contributors to this book are interested in *avodah*, practice. Again and again, they say, return to the work itself, and test it against your own experience. The meditative path teaches that there are two types of faith. The first is when a person sees a friend cross a narrow, rickety bridge. The person thereafter has faith that the bridge can be crossed. The second type of faith is when we "ourselves" cross the bridge. Ah! then we know that we know. We know with our *"kishkes"*; we know from the inside out. This is what the Torah means when it says, "Taste and know that it is good." That is, taste the direct experience of soul, which itself is a piece of the Infinite and is the final text about whether the practice is effective. Meditation is designed to give you direct access to the spiritual. It tolerates no intermediaries.

The purpose of the higher forms of meditation is to break through the masks that deceive us, the lies that hinder us, the ephemeral that depresses us. They seek to move us through normal reality (while never leaving it behind) to actually experiencing the Divine. Additionally, it's important to remember that for Jews, interacting with the world is a component of experiencing the Divine.

A thirteenth-century teacher, Azriel of Gerona, wrote, "One who descends from the root of roots to the form of forms must walk in multiplicity. One who ascends from the form of forms to the root of roots must gather in the multiplicity, for the highest form unites them all, and the root extends through every form that arises from it at any time. When forms are destroyed, the root is not destroyed."[3]

In other words, we are born with choices. To inhabit a body is to be bombarded with various stimuli, each different from the other. This is natural and good. Our task, through our *avodah*, our practice, is to permit all the "forms"—manifestations of self—to be destroyed through deeper consciousness and to realize that there is only one root: Being or God or whatever word is most comfortable to us. We learn to see, embrace, and know that God is One.

The teachers in this book help us to come to that point. They are the midwives of a great blooming.

Meditation from the Heart of Judaism

Rami M. Shapiro is a Reform rabbi and storyteller of Congregation Beth Or in Miami, Florida. He is also the director of The Rasheit Institute for Jewish Spirituality and the author of *Wisdom of the Jewish Sages* and *Minyan: Ten Principles for Living with Integrity.* At first glance, this teaching may seem whimsical—and it is! But there is a deep lesson embedded here, and it offers profound insight into things as they are.

---

1 The Teaching and Practice of Reb Yerachmiel ben Yisrael

RABBI RAMI M. SHAPIRO

A Hasid burst into the study of Reb Yerachmiel ben Yisrael. "Rebbe," he said breathlessly, "what is the way to God?"

The rebbe looked up from his studies and answered, "There is no way to God, for God is not other than here and now."

"Then, Rebbe, tell me the essence of God."

"There is no essence of God, for God is all and nothing."

"Then, Rebbe, tell me the secret that I might know that God is all."

"My friend," Reb Yerachmiel sighed, "there is no way, there is no essence, there is no secret. The truth you seek is not hidden from you. You are hiding from it."

Who is Reb Yerachmiel ben Yisrael? Reb Yerachmiel is me in

moments of spiritual clarity. Reb Yerachmiel comes alive when I meditate and pray, when I sing Hasidic melodies and chant *berachot* (blessings), when I open myself to the depths of Torah and Midrash. Reb Yerachmiel is the rabbi I so want to be and all too rarely am.

When I was asked to participate in this anthology, I knew that I did not belong on these pages. Reb Yerachmiel did. So let me share some of the stories and the teachings of this sage.

THE ALL-NESS OF GOD

"Tell me, Rebbe," a man demanded during Shabbat evening prayers. "Just what is God?" "Tell me," Reb Yerachmiel replied, "just what is not?"

Here, in a sentence, is the heart and soul of my theology. God is All. God is the only Reality. God is the Source of all things and their substance. Thus, we read: "I am God and there is none else" (Isaiah 45:5). Not simply that there is no other God but that there is nothing else but God. "*Adonai* alone is God in heaven above and on earth below; there is none else" (Deuteronomy 4:39). There is nothing else *(ein od)* in heaven or on earth but God.

Some would argue that God is a divine spark inside things. Others would argue that God is a spirit outside things. God is not inside or outside. God is the very thing itself. And when there is no thing, but only empty space? God is that as well.

Picture a bowl in your mind. Define the bowl. Is it just the clay that forms its sides? Or is it the empty space that fills with soup? Without the space, the bowl is not a bowl. Without the side, the bowl is not a bowl. So which is the bowl? The answer is both. To be a bowl, it must have both being and emptiness.

It is the same with God. For God to be God, for God to be All, God must manifest as both being and emptiness. In Hebrew, we call being *yesh*, and we call emptiness *ayin*. And that is what God is: *yesh* and *ayin*.

Being *(yesh)* is that manifestation of God that appears to us as separate entities—physical, spiritual, and psychological. Emptiness *(ayin)* is that manifestation of God that reveals all separation to be illusory: the universe is empty of separate beings.

CREATION IS GOD MADE MANIFEST

"Rebbe," a student asked during a Sabbath retreat, "it is so hard to be whole in this world. I envy those who withdraw and take up the monastic life. Wouldn't we be better off as monks?"

"To withdraw from the world is to withdraw from God," Reb Yerachmiel replied, "for the world is God manifest in time and space."

Consider a magnet that has two poles, one positive and one negative. A magnet cannot be otherwise and still be a magnet. Only when the two poles are together can there be a magnet. Even if you cut the magnet in half and in half again, it will always manifest these two poles. No matter how small you slice the magnet, it requires the duality of positive and negative poles.

Can we say that one pole precedes the other? Can we say that one pole creates the other? Can we say that the poles create the magnet, or that the magnet creates the poles? No. The poles and the magnet are of a greater whole.

Yesh (being) and *ayin* (emptiness) are the poles of God. God cannot be God without them; they cannot be themselves without each other and God. This teaching is called *shlemut,* the nonduality of God, the greater whole encompassing unity and diversity—*ayin* and *yesh.*

Why did God create the world? Because it is God's nature to manifest *yesh* and *ayin,* being and emptiness. Creation is the way God is God in time and space. Thus we read: "Be holy for I, the Source and Substance of all being and emptiness, am holy" (Leviticus 19:2). Holiness is the natural state of creation. We are holy because God is holy, and we are God manifest in time and place. The Torah's command is to be true to our holiness and to honor the holiness of all other things.

HUMANITY'S TASK IS TO KNOW GOD

One morning a group of teenagers asked Reb Yerachmiel, "What is the point of human life? Why are we here?"

The rebbe replied, "If a tree falls in a forest, does it make a sound?" The children debated this for a while, and then the rebbe replied, "Here is my understanding. Without an ear to register the vibrations of the falling tree, no sound is produced. Sound is not a thing but a transaction between things. For there to be sound, there must be a falling tree and an ear to hear. Why are we here? We are the other half of the transaction. We are here to hear."

"But other beings hear!" a student said. "And dogs can hear sounds humans can't hear. Are dogs more important than us?"

"True," Reb Yerachmiel said. "Dogs can hear what we cannot. But we can hear what even dogs cannot. We can hear the cry of a broken heart. We can hear the outrage of injustice. We can hear the whisper of empathy. We can hear the silence of death.

We are here to listen not only to what everyone else can hear, but also to that which only we can hear."

Why are we here? We are here to know God. We are not here to amass fortunes. We are not here to win wars or competitions. We are not here to earn rewards or make for ourselves a great name. We are here to know God and, through our knowing, to transform the world with justice and compassion.

THE ILLUSION OF EVIL

A scholar once approached Reb Yerachmiel at a reception. "Tell me," he said, "if everything is good, where does evil come from?"

Reb Yerachmiel replied, "I do not say that all is good. I say that all is God."

We cannot speak of God and Creation without also speaking of evil. To understand evil, we must understand the nondual nature of God as *yesh* and *ayin*. Thus, we read: "I am the Source and Substance of Reality. There is nothing else. I form light and create darkness. I make peace and create evil. I, the Source and Substance of All, do all this" (Isaiah 45:6–7).

Evil is not the opposite of God; evil is a manifestation of God. What, then, is the purpose of evil? Why does God allow evil to exist? It is not a matter of purpose and allowing; it is a matter of the unconditional nature of God. If God is God, God must contain all possibility, everything and its opposite. Good and evil are but two of the infinite possibilities of God. This does not mean that all evil is inevitable. There are two kinds of evil in the world, necessary and unnecessary, and it is important to distinguish between them.

Necessary evil arises from the transient nature of the world of *yesh,* our everyday world of separate being. Suffering, old age, accident, natural disaster, and death—all the pain that arises from the passing of time and circumstance—these we call "evil" because they thwart our desires and shatter the facade of permanence. In fact, most of what we call "evil" is simply the nature of things in time and space. For all the pain this causes, there is no deliberate evil here.

The proper response to necessary evil is the practice of *avodah be-bittul,* the ending of separate self and permanence through meditation. Free from the illusion of separation and of the idea of permanence, we are able to embrace the natural suffering of impermanent reality with a sense of grace and even humor. We understand that sickness, accidents, the ending of relations (both business and personal), old age, and death are all part of the nature of *yesh.* We do what we can to minimize these, but we do not pretend that we can eliminate them.

Meditation opens us to a deep calm where we can feel fully and respond constructively to whatever life brings. While alive to the tumult of *yesh,* the practitioner of meditation is yet awake to the calm of *ayin.*

Recognizing the inevitability of necessary evil, however, does not excuse the existence of unnecessary evil. Unnecessary evil is what humans do when we act in ways that disrupt unity, foster discord, and promote divisions, hatred, and fear. Unnecessary evil is real evil.

Real evil is those acts of self-gratification that disregard the worth and holiness of other beings. Real evil is generated by a self out of touch with life, a self cut off from God and the compassion, love, and justice that a connection with God releases in us.

What is the antidote to real evil? On a political level, it is justice; on a social level, it is compassion; on a personal level, it is meditation. Unless and until our sense of separateness is opened to our sense of unity, there is no hope for true compassion, justice, or love.

THE NEED FOR "EVIL"

"Isn't it true, rebbe," a student asked during a retreat weekend, "that people are basically good?"

"No," replied Reb Yerachmiel, "people are neither good nor bad, but capable of both."

We are created in the image of God, who manifests as both being and emptiness. Thus we, too, manifest both. In human beings, these appear as *Yetzer Harah* and *Yetzer Hatov.*

Yetzer Hatov is our capacity for unity. It is the power to bridge differences, to build community, to effect harmony.

Yetzer Harah is our capacity to honor differences. *Yetzer Harah* sees diversity where the *Yetzer Hatov* sees oneness. *Yetzer Harah* sees everything apart from everything else; *Yetzer Hatov* sees everything as a part of everything else.

Why call one of these capacities *rah,* "evil"? Because without the balancing insight of the *Yetzer Hatov,* the *Yetzer Harah*'s insistence on separate self and independence pits one life against another, destroying any hope for community, justice, and compassion, all of which rely on understanding our interconnectedness with all things.

Yet a world without *Yetzer Harah* is no less evil. Without the capacity to recognize and respect individual differences, justice is reduced to conformity, compassion to pity, and community to uniformity. Thus, our sages taught that without the *Yetzer Harah*, a person would not marry, build a home, or raise a family, for these rely on our ability to differentiate and celebrate diversity (*Genesis Rabbah* 9:7).

A healthy world needs both *Yetzer Harah,* with its welcoming of and respect for individuality, and *Yetzer Hatov,* with its insight into interdependence and harmony. The human mind contains both inclinations and must use each to balance the other.

AWAKENING TO UNITY

A man grabbed Reb Yerachmiel's arm one *Shabbos* evening after services. "Rebbe, what is the difference between body and soul?"

"None," Reb Yerachmiel said softly. "The body is simply that aspect of the soul visible to the five senses."

We cannot talk of human nature and ignore the soul. Yet our conventional understanding of soul is horribly misguided.

God is both being and emptiness. The former is transient; the latter is timeless. Only the former posits separate selves or souls. The latter knows only oneness. Eternal life in the world to come is a concept arising from the desire of the *Yetzer Harah*, the inclination toward separation and permanence, to deny its eventual and inevitable dissolution in death. Fear of death leads us to imagine separate souls and life eternal in a world to come. In truth, there is none of this.

Sadly, in our efforts to bolster what is ultimately a false sense of self and eternity, we miss the real immortality of which we are a part. *Ayin* (that aspect of reality that is empty of self, soul, and separateness) is deathless, birthless, timeless. And we humans are no less *ayin* than *yesh*.

We are like waves on an ocean. From the surface, each wave appears unique, independent, and transient. Yet beneath the surface, all waves are one, interdependent, and eternal. From the perspective of the wave, there is birth, separation, and death. From the perspective of the ocean, there is no birth, no separation, no death.

From the perspective of *yesh*, we experience birth and death, but from the perspective of *ayin*, we are birthless and deathless. Insofar as we realize the perspective of *ayin*, we are calm, compassionate, and holy. If we focus only on the perspective of *yesh*, we are anxious, frightened, and angry. The challenge is to see ourselves as wave and ocean, *yesh* and *ayin*, simultaneously. The means for doing so is *avodah be-bittul*, meditation, the emptying of the separate self of *yesh* into the oneness of *ayin* and thereby awakening to the greater unity, the perfect nonduality, of God.

QUIETING OURSELVES
TO HEAR OUR SELF

Reb Yerachmiel once traveled to a distant *shul* to teach meditation. The room was packed with students. The rebbe put his finger to his lips and asked the people to be still. "Too noisy," he said after a minute or two. "Please be quiet." The room fell silent. The anxious breathing of the students could be heard. The rebbe waited.

"Shh," he said. "Please, it is still too noisy." The students looked at each other. No one spoke. "Too noisy," Reb Yerachmiel said again. "Too much chatter of the mind. Thoughts, feelings, opinions, judgments. Too much noise. You cannot meditate until you stop the noise. And then you won't have to."

Meditation is a distraction. We imagine that if we learn this or that technique we will become holy. Does Torah say become holy or be holy? It says be holy (Leviticus 19:2). There is no becoming, no need to change, no sense of time, progress, transformation, or journey.

Meditation will not make you holy. You are already holy. Meditation does not make you into someone else; meditation allows you to be who you truly are. Therefore, the psalmist says, "Be still and know that I am God" (Psalm 46:11). If you would be still, quieting body, heart, and mind and opening to the greater silence, then you would know that "I"—the self that you are this very moment—is a manifestation of God.

GIVE THE MIND A BONE

"Rebbe, how can I quiet my mind for meditation?"

"I have a beagle," the rebbe replied, "that never sits still. He is forever scrounging for something to chew on. If I want him to be still, I give him a bone. Then he lays down and chews quietly for hours. The mind is like my beagle. It needs something to chew on."

How do we quiet the mind? I toss mine a bone.

Torah says, "Listen, Israel, the Source and Substance of all Reality is our God, the Source and Substance of all Reality is One....Let these words which I command you today be upon your heart. Repeat them over and over to your children. Speak of them while you sit in your home, while you walk on the way, when you lay down, and when you stand up" (Deuteronomy

6:4–9).

There are only four basic postures a person can take. You are either sitting, standing, walking, or laying down (or some variation of one of these). Torah tells us, then, that in addition to whatever else you may be doing, you should also be repeating *these* words.

What words? Our sages offer many options. I will mention only one. Reb Nachman of Breslov, the great grandson of the Baal Shem Tov, the founder of Hasidic Judaism, taught the repetition of the phrase *Ribbono shel Olam* [lit., "Master of the World"], which I translate as Source and Substance of all Reality. I repeat *Ribbono shel Olam* when I sit in formal meditation, and when I stand for *davvenen* (prayer), when I walk from place to place, and when I lay down to sleep. No matter what I am doing, I am also repeating *Ribbono shel Olam*.

What does this do? Just as my beagle calms down when he has a bone to chew, so my mind calms down when it has something to repeat. In time, it stops chattering altogether, and then I understand the Psalmist, who said, "For You, silence is praise" (Psalm 65).

THE CRYSTAL CANDLESTICK

Once, when speaking to a group in a very fancy synagogue, Reb Yerachmiel was asked, "Rebbe, can you tell me how meditation works?" Without hesitation, the rebbe scooped up a crystal candlestick from the *bimah* and tossed it to the questioner. There was an audible sucking in of frightened breath as everyone focused on the falling crystal. The questioner caught it with a sigh of relief. "That is how meditation works," Reb Yerachmiel said. "The mind becomes focused. There is no thought of this or that, only the task at hand."

We are the content of our minds. Our sense of separateness is a byproduct of our mind's incessant chatter. When I meditate, I allow thoughts and feelings to rise and fall of their own accord. In time, my mind ceases to chatter; self-conscious thought ceases. When thought ceases, self fades; when self fades, time ends; when time ends, eternity reigns. When eternity reigns, there is no *yesh*, only *ayin*; being returns to emptiness, and creation is no more. All is annihilated and empty of separate being.

This is what was meant when the psalmist sang *kalta nafshi,* "my soul is obliterated" (Psalm 84:3). This is what our mystics call *bittul she-me-'ever le-ta'am va-daat,* emptiness beyond reason and knowledge, or, more simply, the end of thought.

With the end of thought and self comes an overwhelming awareness of the unity of all things in God as God. And with this comes a deep sense of compassion and love for Creation. It is this deep love that returns us to the world of *yesh*.

Do not imagine that the end of thought is the end of the matter. For the dissolution of *yesh* into *ayin* is not yet the fullness of God. To fully realize God's *shlemut* (nonduality), we must bring our awareness of emptiness in the world of being. Bringing to bear the love of *ayin*, a selfless love for all things as an extension of God, to bear in the world of seemingly disparate and often desperate things that is *yesh* is the full exercise of meditation. Emptying the self of thought fills the self with love. Filled with love, we cannot but return to the ordinary world of *yesh* and seek to effect *tikkun olam,* repairing the world through love and justice.

FINDING TRUTH BEYOND RELIGION

"Rebbe," a woman asked during an ecumenical panel discussion. "Aren't all religions equally true?"

"No," said Reb Yerachmiel. "All religions are equally false."

The relationship of religion to Truth is like that of a menu to a meal. The menu describes the meal. Yet no matter how exact the description, the menu never becomes the meal. When we mistake the menu for the meal, we do a grave injustice to it and to ourselves. And we do this all the time. Whenever we mistake religion for Truth, imagining that a teaching about God is somehow synonymous with God or becoming so attached to a tradition that we forget the Reality toward which the tradition points, we mistake the menu for the meal.

Religion points beyond itself to a reality that cannot be reduced to words or traditions. The ultimate aim of all authentic religion is to awaken the individual to that Truth beyond religion to which religion points. Authentic religion seeks to awaken you to your unity with God and thereby transform self and society with universal justice and compassion.

It does this in two ways. First, religion posits rules of ethical behavior that help us live as if we were awake even if we are still asleep. This is the right use of the menu. Second, religion teaches some form of meditation leading to the realization of God as the Source and Substance of all and nothing. That is, it leads beyond itself to God.

If a religion leads to nonduality without insisting upon an end to diversity, if it teaches compassion and how to manifest it, if it demands holiness and points the way toward it, then it is good. But, if it holds its truth to be the only truth, if it insists that only its followers are holy, if it alone offers salvation; if it promotes self without teaching selflessness, if its love of God excuses hatred of others and betrayal of Creation, then it is an evil and dangerous faith.

ZEN JUDAISM

A professor once asked, "Aren't you simply dressing Zen in a *tallit* and calling it Judaism?"

Reb Yerachmiel replied, "Truth is Truth. There is no Zen truth or Jewish truth. If something is True, it is true for all. I seek out Truth and share it in my own way. Where do I seek it? In the ordinary experience of my everyday life. Where do I find the words to convey it? In Torah and her commentators. In the Kabbalists, in rebbes. I don't worry that Zen is true. I only worry that I am truthful."

Before we are Jews or Buddhists, we are humans. As humans, we are heirs to the genius of our kind. Krishna, Lao-Tzu, Confucius, Buddha, Jesus, Mohammed, St. Francis, Aurobindo, and Krishnamurti are no less my cousins than Moses, Micah, Hillel, and the Baal Shem Tov. We can learn from all of them, but some will speak more powerfully to us than others.

This is a matter of personal predisposition and parental nurturing. I was raised a Jew, and while I have studied with many teachers, it is Torah that speaks to me most profoundly. For some reason, and I do not pretend to know what that is, I hear the psalmist's "Be still and know" more loudly and more cogently than Buddha's. They may be pointing toward the same Reality, but the finger that guides me best is the one wrapped in tefillin.

THE WAY YOU TEACH

Reb Yerachmiel was walking in his meditation garden as a man approached and demanded, "Rebbe, my rabbi says liberal Judaism stands for nothing. He says it is just an excuse for Jews to be Gentiles. What do you say to that?"

The rebbe replied, "There are only two kinds of Jews, the serious and the not serious. The serious come in many fine flavors. The not serious in only one—bland."

I teach what I call One-Foot Judaism. I take the name from the story of Rabbi Hillel, who was approached by a Gentile who demanded to be taught all of Torah while the great sage stood on one foot. The rabbi balanced himself as requested and then said, "What is hurtful to you, do not do to others. This is the whole of Torah. All the rest is commentary. Go and study it."

Hillel's Judaism had but one pillar; mine has five.

The first is God. Without a sense of God as the nondual Source and Substance of all being and nothingness, Judaism is reduced to ethnicity. Our entire purpose as Jews is to realize godliness in every aspect of our lives. Realizing godliness means that we make the attributes of God the norms of humankind. What are the attributes of God? Mercy, kindness, patience, love, honesty, forgiveness, and justice (Exodus 34:6–7). The serious Jew cultivates these attributes through meditation.

The second pillar is Torah. Torah is the evolving wisdom of the Jews rooted in our sacred texts. Why are these texts sacred? Because they have proved themselves to be accurate guides to godliness. The serious Jew learns basic Hebrew and studies Torah weekly.

The third pillar is Israel. Israel refers to our belonging to the Jewish people. Serious Jews are identified as Jews, placing *mezuzot* on the doorposts of their home, wearing a Magen David around their necks. The serious Jew supports world Jewry and works toward the freedom and dignity of Jews worldwide. The serious Jew upholds the Zionist ideal of the State of Israel as a moral and ethical light unto the nations, visits Israel as an adult, and supports those organizations that make the Zionist ideal a reality.

The fourth pillar is *mitzvot,* behaviors that connect us to God and engage us in acts of godliness. While differing over details, the serious Jew prays or meditates daily, observes Shabbat and the holy days, keeps kosher, and gives *tzedakah* (righteous generosity).

The fifth pillar is *mentschlichkeit,* being a godly human being. Among the obligations that flow from this are *gemilut chesed* (practicing kindness), *teshuvah* (self-evaluation and ethical perfection), working for *tikkun olam* (repairing the world through justice and compassion), visiting the sick, and avoiding hurtful speech.

PRAYER OR MEDITATION?

A woman came to Reb Yerachmiel and said, "I have been studying with a Buddhist teacher who has given me clear instructions as to how to meditate. I find it very helpful. I told this to my rabbi, and he got angry with me, claiming I am abandoning my faith. He said I should cease my meditation and learn to pray. Rebbe, what do you think I should do?"

Reb Yerachmiel replied, "Your rabbi is half right. You should learn to pray. And what should you pray? Just this: Dear God, grant me the courage to stick with my meditation."

While meditation is essential to spiritual life, it is not sufficient. I teach a ten-point program of spiritual practice called
Minyan. The first point is *avodah be-bittul,* meditation—silent
sitting twenty to thirty minutes each morning to open the
boundaries of *yesh* (separate being) to the greater oneness of
ayin (emptiness and unity). The second is *Gerushin,* recitation
of a sacred phrase. I recite Reb Nachman's *Ribbono shel Olam*
during meditation and throughout the day. Third is *Musar,* daily
study of teachings that help me to be holy.

Fourth is *kavvanah,* focused attention. I punctuate my day
with moments of soft breathing and silent recitation of *Ribbono
shel Olam,* which help me attend more fully to the task at hand.
Fifth is *teshuvah,* self-perfection—taking time each evening to
assess my behavior and see what I can do to make tomorrow a
little more kind and just than today. Sixth is *tzedakah,* generosity—making sure that I give three to ten percent of my income
to people or organizations in need. Seventh is *gemilut chesed,*
random acts of loving-kindness—consciously seeking opportunities to be of service to others.

Eight is *pitron chalomot,* dreamworld. Dreams often contain spiritual lessons that cannot be made conscious any other
way. I keep a pad, pen, and penlight by my bed and jot down
my dreams upon waking. I study them as I would a text of Torah, looking for deeper meanings and insights. Ninth is *kashrut,*
ethical consumption. I cannot live without consuming life, so I
take care to live lightly and well—eating lower on the food chain,
shopping wisely, maintaining a healthy body and mind, and
attending to the health of mother earth. Tenth is Shabbat, setting aside the seventh day for mindfulness, living one day as I
would like to live every day—with attention, justice, and kindness.

THE COLD SHOWER OF REALITY

During a retreat on spirituality, a woman rose and said, "I have no need of these practices. I feel spiritual all the time without doing anything."

Reb Yerachmiel looked at her for a moment and said, "The next time you have a spiritual feeling, take a cold shower. Then dry off and do something kind for someone else."

Spirituality is not a feeling. Spirituality is paying attention. Spirituality is being present to what is happening around and within you regardless of how you feel. Spirituality is living in the world with kindness, compassion and justice even when you feel like doing otherwise.

Spirituality is not different from everyday life. It is doing everyday things with a clear and attentive mind. Doing everyday things with a clear and attentive mind awakens us to the fact that we are both apart from and a part of everything else. We discover that from the perspective of *Yesh*, we are unique, irreducible, irreplaceable manifestations of God. We discover from the perspective of *Ayin* that we are totally interconnected with and dependent upon all other manifestations of God. We are awake to our being and our emptiness simultaneously. And from this we awake to God, the Source and Substance of both.

✳

Lawrence Kushner, a Reform rabbi, is the spiritual leader of Congregation Beth El in Sudbury, Massachusetts. The author of *Invisible Lines of Connection: Sacred Stories of the Ordinary, Honey from the Rock: An Easy Introduction to Jewish Mysticism,* and other books that help people understand Jewish spirituality, Rabbi Kushner approaches the problem of the inner noise we all experience when we try to meditate. His concern is how to deal with this, how to calm it, and how to release it into God.

---

2   Silencing the Inner Voice(s)

RABBI LAWRENCE KUSHNER

If we had a keen vision and feeling for all ordinary human life, it would be like hearing the grass grow, the squirrel's heart beat, and we should die of that roar which lies on the other side of silence.

—*George Eliot*

My favorite part of sailing comes about fifteen minutes into the voyage, after we've loaded all our gear aboard, removed all the covers, freed all the lines, pumped the bilge, checked the safety equipment, opened the seacocks, turned "on" the batteries, started the engine, cast off the mooring line, negotiated our way through the boats in the harbor, raised the main, unfurled the jib, trimmed the sails, set a course—then the moment comes. I reach down to the throttle and pull it back all the way and shut off the fuel to the diesel. In a second or two, the engine sputters to a stop. Now, except for the whisper of the wind in the sails and the gurgle of water rushing past the hull, there is only silence. Saying anything now would damage the serenity of the moment.

For me, there is a metaphor here that begs attention. The silence comes, but its preamble is tremendous busyness and noise. We humans are far better at making noise than silence. But silence is better than noise. Indeed, attaining silence may just be the reason for prayer. I don't mean just not talking; I mean also stilling the inner dialogue. And, as in so much Jewish spirituality, this is taught through carefully examining sacred text.

VOICE UTTERING ITSELF

We have a fascinating irregularity in Numbers 7:89. After all the princes of Israel have brought their gifts of consecration, Moses is left alone in the newly completed wilderness tabernacle. The text reads: "[Moses] heard the Divine Voice speaking to him...." Given the context, that does not seem especially noteworthy. A very close reading, however, turns up one extraneous grammatical dot. Normally, the word for speaking, *midabbaer*, appears in the *piel* conjugation with a dot, or *dagesh*, in the middle root letter, which is *bet*. But curiously here, in addition to the one in the letter *bet*, the *dalet* is also vocalized with a *dagesh* (a dot) of its own. And, if the conjugation is *piel*, that dot is not supposed to be there.

Rashi, a wonderful medieval commentator, explains that the reason for this irregularity is that the verb *midabbaer* is actually an odd form of what used to be *midabbaer*. It is a *hitpael* grammatical form with an assimilated letter *heh*. All that now remains of the *heh* is the *dagesh*. And this renders the verse not "[Moses] heard the Divine Voice speaking to him," but "[Moses] heard the Voice uttering itself." Moses overheard the Divine Self uttering itself. But if the Divine Self is uttering itself and the Divine Self is also the source of yourself, then who is listening?

SPEAKER OF THE SELF

Did you ever talk to yourself? I don't mean when you were alone in the car. I mean did you ever ask yourself a question to find out if you knew the answer? Like, "Who am I?" or "What is the meaning of my life?" Did you ever get an answer? What would you do if the answer was, "Who wants to know?" In other words, when you talk to yourself, who's talking and who's listening?

The fact that we can hold these interior conversations with our "selves" means that we are fragmented, alienated, broken. If we were whole, then there could be no conversation because there would be no one else in there to talk to.

Such self-reflecting mind games are the enemy of religious experience. In film or drama, this is called "breaking the third wall." The actor suddenly turns to the camera and speaks to it as if it were a real person. He jars the viewers into realizing they are only watching a movie. The spell is broken.

Menachem Mendl of Kotzk, a nineteenth-century Hasidic teacher, deliberately misreads Deuteronomy 5:5, in which Moses says, "*Anochi omed bayn Adonai u'vaynaykhem,*" "I stood between God and you." Menachem Mendl teaches that it is your I, "your ego that stands between you and God. Normally not even an iron barrier can separate Israel from God, but self-preoccupation and ego will drive them apart."[1]

In other words, when we do something with all of ourselves, we're not aware we're doing it. There is no one in there to hear it. The part of our consciousness that normally tells the rest of us that we are present is busy doing it, too. As Buckaroo Banzai said, "Wherever you go, there you are."

DANCING ON THE ROPE

Rabbi Hayyim of Krosno, a disciple of the Baal Shem Tov, once stopped with his students to watch a man dance on a rope strung high between two buildings. Rabbi Hayyim became so absorbed in the spectacle that his Hasidim asked him what he found so fascinating in such a frivolous circus performance.

"I can't get over it," he explained. "This man is risking his life, and I am not sure why. I am sure that while he is walking on the rope, he cannot be thinking about the hundred gulden he is earning. He cannot be thinking about the step he has just taken or the step he is going to take next. He cannot even be thinking about where is. If he did, he would fall to his death. He must be utterly unaware of himself!"[2]

When we're "dancing on the rope," our inner conversation ceases and we realize that our sense of self is actually an obstacle. It renders us observers of our own lives. It tricks us into thinking that our self is somehow other than who we are. There is only one of you in there and out here, and it's the same one. The business of serious religion is to get you to abolish the distinctions between inside and outside, between observer and observed. The goal is to be fully present in whatever you do, just like God is in the world.

WANTING WHAT GOD WANTS

"If mysticism is the quintessence of religion," as Moshe Idel says in *Kabbalah: New Perspectives,* then "the quintessence of mysticism is the sense of union with God."[3] In Judaism, "union with God" is called *devekut,* or literally, "cleaving." The classic sources of *devekut* are Deuteronomy 4:4, "but you that cleave [*had'vaykim*] unto the Lord your God this day are alive everyone of you this day," and Isaiah 43:11, "*Anochi Adonai Anochi,*" "I, I am the Lord,"[4] where the first 'I' is God and the second is the self. And the famous line at the burning bush, "*Ehyeh Asher Ehyeh,*" of Exodus 3:14, which is usually rendered, "I will be who I will be," but I interpret to mean "I will be who you are!"

We don't want to just read about what God wants. We don't want someone else telling us what God wants, either. We don't even want God telling us what God wants. We want our eyes to be God's eyes so that we can see the world the way God sees it. We want our teaching to be God's Torah. We want our hands to do God's work. We want our prayers to be God's prayers. We want to want what God wants.

DEVEKUT: BEING ONE WITH GOD

Devekut, Unio Mystica, gives us a new handle on a whole genre of statements that have always seemed both holy and heretical at the same time. For example, Rabbi Dov Baer of Mezritch advised his students that "...the best way to teach Torah...[is to be only] an ear listening to how the world of speech speaks through [you]....[When you] begin to hear your own words, ...stop."[5] The Baal Shem Tov says, "When I fix my thoughts on the Creator, I let my mouth speak what it will, for the words are bound to the higher roots."[6] And Kalonymos Kalmish Shapira of Piesetzna, who perished in the Warsaw Ghetto, explained, "Not only does God hear our prayers, God prays them through them as well."[7]

Idel identifies three forms of *devekut*.[8] He begins with what he calls Aristotelian *devekut*, in which, during the act of cognition, the knower and the known become one. Idel cites Rabbi Ezra of Gerona who said, "The ancient pious men caused their thought to ascend to the place of its source, and they would recite the *mitzvot* and the [Ten] Commandments and through this recitation and this cleaving of thought...they received a [divine] influx from the annihilation of thought."[9] This describes the experience of the loss of self by someone who is cerebral, rational, linear, whose left brain is dominant.

A second mode of *devekut* Idel terms the "theurgic." I would call it the *devekut* of "behavior." In this experience, the Jew seeks to literally affect God through specific actions. The *devekut* of behavior is predicated on the structural similarity and interdependence of the human body with the supernal image of God in the *sefirot*.[10] (*Sefirot* is a kabbalistic term that refers to the ten elements or stages of God's presence in the world. They are the constituent parts of God's being, as it were.) As Menachem Nahum of Chernobyl taught, "Commandment...is called *mitzvah* because it joins together the part of God that dwells within the person with the infinite God beyond. It may be, then...that [the *mitzvah*] contains the *Shechinah* [literally "resting" or "dwelling," the Divine Presence and feminine aspect of God], and in fulfilling it one has both [commandment and presence]."[11] In this mode of *devekut*, your will and each of your deeds become God's. If you become a servant of God, then your action is God's action. By repairing things here, we repair them above. A personality drawn to such *devekut* is action oriented, content neither with study nor with meditation. This personality is a doer, an achiever, a fixer, someone who wants to repair the world. If the first personality was a "head person," the second would be a "hands person."

Idel associates the third and last form of *devekut* with Neoplatonism. Its adherents are primarily concerned with reuniting the soul with its root. They draw heavily on the imagery of transformation, ascent, and return. I call this the *devekut* of prayer. In describing this mode, Idel cites the words of an anonymous fourteenth-century Kabbalist: "The soul of the righteous one will ascend—while he is yet alive—higher and higher, to the place where the souls of the righteous [enjoy their] delight, which is the cleaving of the mind."[12] The focus of this third personality is neither cerebral nor behavioral but emotional. Such a soul is drawn to closing his eyes, to losing herself in song, to sitting in silence. This is a "heart person."

THE ONE WHO ASKS
IS THE ONE WHO HEARS

We can now reconsider the strange case of the extra *dagesh* (dot) in Numbers 7:89 and the question with which we began of how to stop being self-conscious. In the words of Rabbi Nachman of Breslov, "The core of a human being is his consciousness. Where one's consciousness is, there is the whole person. Thus one who knows and reaches an understanding of the divine is really in the divine. The greater one's knowing, the more fully is he included in his root in God."[13]

I am convinced that *devekut* is more than being one with God. *Devekut* is a theological metaphor for stopping the dialogue between the two inner voices. *Devekut* is a metaphor for self-unification. *Devekut* is a time when the outer person is revealed to be illusory, a figment of the language, an iron barrier separating us from God. Now only an unselfconscious awareness remains, an awareness that bears a wonderful similarity to the Divine. On Yom Kippur, a woman in my congregation offered a personal prayer in which she prayed for the wisdom to "wish to be who she was."

Devekut is when the one who asks and the one who hears become the same. We realize to our embarrassment that we have been who we were all along and that it was only linguistic convention that tricked us into thinking we were someone else. We cannot make God do what we want, but in thinking, doing, and praying what God wants, we become one with God and with ourselves.

✳

Alan Lew is a Conservative rabbi and spiritual leader of Congregation Beth Shalom in San Francisco. Coming to Judaism and the rabbinate after many years of Zen Buddhism gives Rabbi Lew a unique perspective. His prime interest is to *get on with the work*. While many Jewish leaders argue about the age and lineage of Jewish meditation, Rabbi Lew teaches that concrete practice is what needs to be embraced. The particulars will work themselves out.

---

3   It Doesn't Matter What You Call It: If It Works, It Works

RABBI ALAN LEW

Why do we meditate? I do it in response to the call I feel from my deepest inner being. The call carried me to Buddhism many years ago, and Buddhist meditation helped me hear the call with such clarity that I eventually heard it say, "Don't be a Buddhist anymore. Become a Jew."

It is this call that now leads me to synthesize the very useful practices I learned during my 10 years in Buddhism with the very deep and soul-satisfying practice of Judaism. For me, this is what a spiritual quest is all about, and it is what meditation can help us do. When we go back to the deepest and earliest strata of Judaism (which is to say the Torah), we find a kind of typology of the human encounter with the Transcendent. In the Torah, one human being after another encounters God. If you put all these experiences together, a model of this experience emerges. A striking feature of this encounter is leave-taking. Most significant encounters with God in the Torah begins with *vayetze* (go out, exit) or *lech lecha* (get going!) or some such leave-taking. With Moses, we find a *double* leave-taking. First, he flees Egypt for Midian, then he leaves everybody in Midian and goes to the farthest point of an isolated wilderness. The story of the Exodus of the Jewish people from Egypt—*Yetziat Mitzraim*, the greatest leave-taking in all history—is clearly a prerequisite to the great epiphany at Sinai. Every experience of God begins with leaving one's ordinary way of perceiving the world. We must leave the way we are comfortable and enter a more vulnerable and open state. We must enter the state where we are naked. That's where we encounter God.

I'm not sure whether we can—or should—"stay" in this place, although we can certainly visit it in a regular, disciplined way. So the value of meditation practice is that it represents a leave-taking. In fact, in the Jewish mystical tradition, this is the original meaning of the word *Hitbodedut* meditation, which means "to go" or "be alone." Meditation always involves a kind of leave-taking till we come home.

THE VARIETIES OF TRANSFORMATIVE EXPERIENCE

The second striking feature of the biblical encounter with the Transcendent is that it always involves a transformation. Basically there are three kinds of transformation.

The first is reflected in a sense of place and reality. We feel the spiritual base of our environment. This is the experience of Jacob's *vayetze* (going out) experience: When he had the vision of the ladder planted on the earth and reaching up to heaven, then woke up the next morning saying, "God was in this place, and I knew it not" (Genesis 28:16).

The second kind of experience occurs when we transform our understanding of our own self and our personal, inner reality. This is reflected in the wrestling match with the angel in which Jacob's name became Yisrael and his experience of himself was deepened. Jacob was always chasing after the heel of another person. Through his "wrestling," he came to accept this quality in himself in a very deep way.

The third aspect of transformation is entering the realm of the transcendent: being aware of God and of the Ultimate Ground of Being. In the Torah, this occurs most clearly in Moses' burning bush experience. Here, Moses asks God for His name and is told, "*Ehyeh asher ehyeh*," "I will be what I will be." Later on, God is named with the letters *yod heh vav heh*. Both names indicate absolute, unconditional Being. This, to me, is the most powerful potential of meditation: entering fully into God.

Hebrew is a very interesting language. The only way you can say "to be" in the present tense is by saying the most widely used Name of God—*yod heh vav heh*. There is no verb. When you say "I am cold" in Hebrew, you say "I cold." You cannot say "am," since there is no word for "am"—*except* God. And so, to me, meditation approaches this sense of Absolute Being *in the present tense*.

If the point of meditation is to experience your reality more deeply, not everyone will want to do it. But I don't think it presents a danger to anyone, and the healing potential of being more present with one's reality is universal. I don't believe anyone would not benefit from this. But clearly, many people will not choose to do so. Most of the meditations that I lead at my synagogue are clearly identified as "meditation," but occasionally I will introduce meditation at a larger service, such as the High Holy Days, that basically consists of a period of silence. I do not label this "meditation." Many people are frightened of meditation, and many do not wish to confront their reality this way and to see themselves more clearly. So when I meditate with a large, randomly chosen group, people may be giggling or doing anything they can to avoid having even a single moment of silence. Silent self-confrontation can be very frightening to some people, but you can't force somebody past that fear.

THE VARIETIES OF MEDITATIVE EXPERIENCE

To me, there are three fundamental kinds of meditation: (1) relaxation meditation, the primary purpose of which is relaxation; (2) trance-meditation, in which one "leaves" one's ordinary state of mind; and (3) transformative meditation, which involves fully inhabiting one's own experience. The third is the kind of spiritual activity that has always proved most fruitful for me. I've done quite a bit of trance-meditation, and I have a weakness for it; I enjoy it. But I don't find it to be as spiritually fruitful, in the long run, as transformative meditation.

In the Jewish contemplative tradition, there are many varieties of meditation. The *Hasidim Rishonim* (the early Hasidim who exemplified meditation practice and sweetness of heart) used to simply sit for an hour before praying so they could attune their hearts and minds to the activity of prayer. This is an example of awareness meditation. In Kabbalah, particularly in ecstatic Kabbalah and in the kinds of practices that came out from Abraham Abulafia, the thirteenth-century Kabbalist and meditation teacher, there are a lot of trance-inducing kinds of meditation. But overall, Jewish mysticism focuses on the present moment.

I see myself as part of the nontrance school. I use my contemplative practice to encounter the Divine through directly experiencing reality rather than leaving that experience and going elsewhere in trance. To me, this has always been the real power of meditation.

Meditation can deepen our experience of Jewish ritual, which is precisely what's needed right now because mainstream Judaism knows the words but seems to have lost the song. Meditation can join the music back with the words.

The Mishnah (the first comprehensive book of Jewish law—a compilation of laws, custom and ethical teaching) says that you shouldn't stand to pray unless you're in a state called *khoved rosh* ("weighted head"). This is usually very inadequately translated as "unless you're serious." It is a warning that you shouldn't fool around when you pray. The *Hasidim Rishonim* sat for an hour before praying to produce a state of *khoved rosh*. The *shoresh* (the root of the word) of *khoved* is "weight." It suggests that meditation can make your head "weightier," that it can make your consciousness denser. This is the real power of meditation. Once we're in a state of dense consciousness, prayer becomes a richer, deeper, denser experience.

Norman Fisher, the abbot of the San Francisco Zen Centers, and I were foot-soldier Zen students together for about ten years. Then I went to rabbinical school at the Jewish Theological Seminary. Norman has an Orthodox background. When he was a kid, he used to *davven* every day and study Talmud with his rabbi in the little Pennsylvania town where he grew up. Once he visited me at the seminary. In those days, we had a very traditional minyan. About fifty people would *davven* every morning, and all of them knew the service quite well. It was a very powerful minyan. Norman walked in and just shocked me. He started *davvening* as if he'd never missed a day in his life. I was stunned because I'd never seen this in him. I had known about it only as a distant, intellectual idea. But here was Norman, whom I'd known as a Zen student for our entire relationship, swaying in prayer, wearing *tefillin* (small ritual boxes filled with prayer that are worn on the body while praying), and walking out of the seminary with a radiance I never even saw at Tassajara, a Zen center in California, where we had meditated for three straight months. He said to me, "You know Alan, now that I've done Zen meditation, I could *davven* for the rest of my life, and it would be enough. I wouldn't have to do anything else. But if I hadn't done Zen meditation, I wouldn't even know what this is."

That line has been my motto for the last five years. I lead meditation groups four times a week before the prayer service in the hope of somehow replicating the experience that Norman and I had: letting meditation open us to Judaism's very profound spirituality. I may sit in my daily minyan and have a very profound experience, and a new person is sitting six inches away who has come in the hope of having such an experience, also. But he's not having it, and he is angry—angry at Judaism, angry at me, angry at the synagogue. Somehow, he doesn't have access to the very profound spirituality of ordinary Jewish ritual.

IS MEDITATION A JEWISH TRADITION?

There is a great debate over whether Judaism has a tradition of meditation. I am very squarely in the indifferent camp. Almost certainly there is, but many people have a different opinion. Still, it seems to be an almost completely irrelevant question. We don't have to *kasher* meditation. Many forms of meditation do not threaten or oppose Jewish theology. There's no reason why we can't assimilate them into Jewish practice, whether or not there's a Jewish precedent for them. Judaism assimilated aspects of the ancient Near Eastern oral tradition into the Torah, Greek tradition into the Talmud, and the Sufi or pre-Sufi Arabic tradition into Kabbalah. The Rambam was completely audacious with his use of Aristotelian philosophy. As a friend once said to me, "Judaism seems to have a kind of cell-like mechanism. We seem to know intuitively what it can absorb and what's toxic." To me, meditation that involves visualizing deities or reciting Hindu mantras would be toxic to Judaism. But a simple awareness exercise, a meditation which helps penetrate our experience of reality through becoming more aware of our breath and posture and our thought processes, would not under any circumstances be toxic to Judaism. Therefore, I have no problem adopting such techniques.

Praying with *kavvanah* doesn't feel different than when I am in deep meditation. However, it's clearly an experience with a different *objective*—and certainly a whole different mode of expression. But the feelings seem almost identical. Standing during the *Amidah* feels no different to me than when I am in deep awareness meditation.

I am not sanguine about the role of Kabbalah in the renewal of Jewish spirituality. Kabbalah does have its uses, for it provides a language for talking about the inner Judaism that we have been unable to talk about for far too long. But I think the actual practice of Kabbalah is simply not a realistic or attainable goal for the vast majority of American Jews. Kabbalah is extremely difficult and complex. It depends on a rigorous pattern of Jewish observance and on the mastery of the most difficult Torah study skills—not only Hebrew, but also Aramaic and Gemarah. But, the vast majority of Jews who are in need of spiritual renewal these days are neither observant not educated. People want to fly, but they haven't even tried crawling yet. I studied Talmud for six years at the seminary and I was very good at it, but when I studied Kabbalah, I could barely follow my teacher. I felt as if I was holding on for dear life. Authentic Kabbalah cannot be simplified or translated. It is based on the Hebrew language—in many cases, on the letters themselves—and when we endeavor to translate Kabbalah, we usually end up merely talking about it rather than practicing it. This is mostly what passes for Kabbalah these days—people talking about it a great deal and not really doing it, a highly watered-down activity without much potential for spiritual transformation.

I think we need to start out on a more basic level. I think that what people really need these days is to be opened to *normative* Judaism—to Shabbat and to daily prayer—and I think that simple awareness meditation has the capacity to accomplish this. Meditation opens us to the inner richness of whatever we are doing.

WAKING UP YOUR LIFE

How does one start a Jewish meditation practice? First, it's important to sit with other people. There are many strictures against doing too much meditation by yourself. If you meditate by yourself, you can fall prone to the delusion of Self and become focused on your own personal relationship with God.

When you *davven* with a *kehilla* (a group of like-minded people), you are part of a communal address to God. That's really the only way to meditate because, spiritually speaking, being an "individual" is to me a materialist myth.

Also, if at all possible, you should learn how to meditate from people who know how to do it. The technique of meditation is very important: how you hold your body, how you relate to your breath, the subtle difference between controlling your breath and not controlling it, being aware of your breath without manipulating or forcing it. All around the country, there are increasingly abundant opportunities to learn these skills. Right now, seven of the eight largest Conservative synagogues in northern California have regular meditation groups. The most difficult thing about meditation for American Jews is the discipline required to do it. Fixed in the American psyche is the idea that spirituality is a leisure activity, something you do on the weekend. We've really lost the sense of disciplined spirituality. Some people come to my groups and get really excited for a while. Then they stop coming regularly. Then they stop coming completely. So this sense of spiritual discipline is essential to the practice.

Another problem is that there is a tendency for people to look elsewhere for their satisfaction. They may worship the exotic or the external or what is foreign to their own experience. But when they start to meditate, they quickly confront these aspects of their cultural conditioning because meditation—at least the kind that I advocate—carries you directly into your experience. The kind of meditation I do allows experience to rise up, and then you let go of it. But people raised in our culture are not good at letting go.

When we meditate, we condition ourselves to directly

experience reality. If we make a habit of doing this, it spills over into the rest of our lives, and we suddenly find ourselves doing it constantly. If we are walking down the street, for instance, suddenly the street is beautiful and the quality of light is extraordinary and the sound is a miraculous symphony. One such moment every day—one moment of consciousness, of wakefulness—can transform your life completely. Such moments over the course of the day will become more pronounced. Eventually, they will be the moments around which your life is centered. And suddenly, you will find yourself waking up to your life. This is the kind of consciousness that transforms us. This is a system that wakes you up to your experience, to the ordinary miracle of being alive. This, to me, is the deepest joy of Judaism and is the potential of meditation as well.

✳

Susie Schneider teaches meditation and Jewish mysticism in Jerusalem. She is the founder of a correspondence school called A Still Small Voice, which instructs its students in the practice of Torah and *mitzvot* as a spiritual path. In this teaching, she presents Torah study as a method of Jewish meditation often ignored by contemporary teachers. She explores both how to study meditatively and how meditation can strengthen study.

---

4   Study as Meditation

SUSIE SCHNEIDER

The service of meditation is the spiritual and intellectual quest to know, comprehend, and feel an idea or truth of Torah to the fullest extent possible. By pursuing a matter to its depth, one draws his inherited and instinctive knowledge of God into a more revealed and conscious state. The purpose of meditation is to train a person to perceive reality more correctly.

> — *Rabbi Yitzchok Ginsburgh, a contemporary teacher of Kabbalah*

Meditation is a continuous flow of thought upon a particular object or point of focus.

> —*Patanjali, a medieval yoga philosopher*

Any regular meditation practice, whether of Eastern, Western, Jewish, or personal design, frees the mind from its bondage to surface layers and directs it to experience the infinite depth that is always available in each moment.

Every meditation has a point of focus. It could be a mantra such as a name of God or the *Sh'ma* or another meaningful affirmation. It could be an object such as a geometric image, a scribal design, or even a candle. It could be one's breath or the stillness that lies within each moment. It could even be an intellectual question about the nature of reality or the significance of some ritual law or how to apply Torah principles to a present problem.

When first learning to meditate, it is easier to choose a simple and concise object of focus—a single and static word, an image, or a point of the body. The idea is to fix your mind on it for a set length of time. When your mind wanders, return its focus gently but firmly to the object of meditation. As you grow more skilled in this practice, it becomes possible to choose more complex and nonstatic subjects. In this sense, text study is a more advanced meditation. To do it properly, you must already know how to bring yourself into a meditative alpha state with ease. (An alpha state is a brain wave pattern and psychological state that characterize deep relaxation and are associated with meditation.)

THE LIGHTS OF STUDY ARE THE LIGHTS OF SINAI

The purpose of meditation is to expand and strengthen consciousness. Its goal is often called "en*light*enment." As the mind stretches, it is able to hold more "light." In Jewish writings, *light* and *consciousness* are equivalent terms.

Text study as meditation enables the mind to directly re-access that intense revelation of light and consciousness that happened at Sinai. The Cosmic Mind reveals its truths and secrets in many ways to many people, both individually and collectively. The circumstances and magnitude of the Torah's transmission to the Jewish people are unique in history. This tremendous revelation was received through a group *samadhia* (a Sanskrit word that indicates the direct experience of God, also called "realization" and sometimes "prophesy"). Six hundred thousand family units (estimated at two million people) simultaneously experienced the revelation of the Torah at Sinai. The entire nation of Israel "saw" the Presence of God and perceived Divine truths at the same time:

> And it came to pass on the third day in the morning, that there were thunders and lightning, and a thick cloud upon the mountain, and the sound of a shofar exceedingly loud; so that all the people in the camp trembled. And Moses brought the people out of the camp to meet with God; and they stood at the foot of the mountain. And Mount Sinai smoked in every part, because the Lord descended upon it in fire; and the smoke of it ascended like the smoke of a furnace, and the whole mountain quaked greatly. And then the voice of the shofar sounded louder and louder; Moses spoke and God answered him by a voice....And God spoke these words saying, "I am the Lord your God, who brought you out of the land of Egypt, out of the house of bondage. You shall have no other gods beside me...." And all the people perceived the thunderings, and the lightning, and the sound of the shofar, and the mountain smoking; and when the people saw it they were shaken, and stood afar off. (Exodus 19:16–18; 20:1–3,18)

The light accessed through text study provides us with the pure light of Sinai, undiluted and unattenuated. It is a thick, sweet, blissful light that fills our soul, our heart, and our bones. The text of the Torah itself as well as all of the writings that it has spawned has this power to link back to the fire of Sinai.

Text study as meditation emphasizes the following effects:

* It is extremely potent in developing and rectifying intuition.
* One attains a deep and internalized understanding of the nature and structure of reality, for "the Torah is the mind of God."
* One achieves deep and passionate cleaving to God that Kabbalah calls the union of "kisses" that unites "breath to Breath."
* It is not only a meditation but also a *mitzvah* and so enjoys the benefits of both; each rectifying a different level of soul. (The term *mitzvah* refers to the 613 actions specified by the Torah as obligatory or forbidden. With six notable exceptions, a *mitzvah* always requires some physical activity for its fulfillment.)

MITZVAH AND MEDITATION AS COMPLEMENTARY MODES OF SERVICE

When first comparing meditation and *mitzvah*, it seems that meditation would penetrate more deeply into the unconscious, while the effects of *mitzvot* (as gross physical actions) would stop at the superficial layers of being. Action appears as a surface-oriented practice when compared to meditation's more inner and subtle stirrings of soul. Yet, in terms of *tikkun* (reparation), the opposite is true: *mitzvah* actually penetrates more deeply into the unconscious than meditation.

The primary benefit of meditation is that it expands and enhances consciousness by strengthening focus and concentration. When people are easily distracted, they do not penetrate into the depths of things, and consequently their conduct lacks mindful intent. Such individuals are driven by their unconscious because they do not examine its impulses and question its intentions. Only by mindful discrimination between life-enhancing and life-undermining urges does the lower nature loose its ruling grip. Meditation practice corrects and expands people's perception of reality and encourages them to change according to their broadening awareness of truth. Though meditation extends the boundaries of conscious awareness to include more and more of what had previously been unconscious, its primary field of influence remains the conscious realms of heart and mind. The unconscious, to the extent that it remains unconscious, can only be rectified by right action.

The unconscious, called the *nefesh*, is identified with the animal or vital soul, for it performs the vital functions of the body: it keeps the blood circulating, the cells dividing, the lungs expanding, the stomach churning. It is also responsible for such elementary emotions as the fight-or-flight response, sexual arousal, territoriality, and familial loyalties. In other words, it directs all the functions we have in common with our fellow creatures in the animal kingdom.

The animal soul has an animal world-view. It is concerned with creature comforts and physical security and will sacrifice anything to satisfy those needs. The Divine soul, on the other hand, wants only to serve God and is equally adamant in its pursuit. It, too, will gladly forego anything, even life itself, to draw closer to its Creator.

Meditation calms, but does not transmute, the animal level of self. This is accomplished only by action, by forcing the animal soul to actively serve the Divine. We employ the same technique to train the animal soul as one would use to train an actual animal. Through forced repetition of appropriate behavior, the trainer impresses a habit of right action on the animal. Similarly, the *mitzvot* habituate our animal souls to behave in spiritually productive ways.

The 613 *mitzvot* reveal the science of right action for the human kingdom. Each *mitzvah* defines a physical act that must be performed by the animal soul and repeated time and again. In this way, the body gets programmed to act in accordance with spiritual law as defined by Torah.

"Greased pathways" is the term that scientists use to describe the neurological effects of *mitzvah* practice. Every time a person performs a particular deed, they "grease" that neural pathway, making it more likely that the same deed will happen again. Now, at a crossroads where several options exist, the alternative already tried is more likely to happen again. And even more so the next time. That option has been "greased." The image is graphic. Imagine a number of children's slides all branching out from a common center. If one is greased and the others not, it will quickly become the preferred option.

Each *mitzvah* "greases" a pathway and effects a physiological transformation in the person who performs it. In the course of a lifetime of *mitzvah* practice, a complete network of neural pathways gets wired into the body.

Judaism teaches that our souls come into this world primarily to rectify the animal level of self. The Divine soul is already perfect and is immune to the contaminating effects from wrong living, so the priority is to refine our animal souls by training them to serve God and obey spiritual law. The primary tool for this work is *mitzvah* practice. Through it, the "wild beast" acquires healthy instincts. Its animal nature is neither denied nor abrogated; it is simply cleaned of shortsighted and self-defeating habit patterns.

Text study, because it combines both *mitzvah* and meditation, is a uniquely powerful tool of transformation. Its requirement of focused concentration on the text in an alternation of still-mind and active-mind is a potent meditation technique. Its practice of voicing the words aloud and dialoguing with a study partner engages the body's vocal organs, thereby greasing neural pathways and engraving habits of right speech.

GUIDES FOR MAKING TORAH STUDY A MEDITATION PRACTICE

✳ You must approach Torah learning with a deep and sincere desire to be transformed by God's will and its Truth. Ideally, this intention should be articulated as an actual prayer before study.

✳ Find (or create) a place within you that is burning to understand what this text is teaching because you know that your "life" depends upon it, that it holds a key to your quality of life. The measure of your drive to know will be the measure of your willingness to work, for our sages teach, "the reward (i.e., benefit of a spiritual practice) is only proportionate to the labor."

✳ The means *are* the ends. Release all expectations of covering a certain amount of pages or of getting to the end of a text within a certain amount of time. Each sentence (sometimes each word) has its own treasure. Even if it is just restating a previous idea, you must seek to experience it now, in this moment, as a new revelation. You should get excited by the concept each time you hear it. You should feel stretched and delighted anew by its depth. After each sentence, ask yourself, "What do I know now that I didn't know before?" Stay in the present. All meditation trains us to access the depth of each moment.

* After each new idea, recap the logical development of the piece. Go back to the beginning, and follow it through, adding this next piece of information on to the end. The recap becomes a mantra that triggers new associations.

* You must be rigorously precise in your translation. Look up all unfamiliar words, as well as all biblical, talmudic, and midrashic citations. Your understanding the text's most basic level of sense becomes the vessel that draws the creative insight. If this stage is sloppy and superficial, it will not pull a clean light.

* Go through each text at least three times, discovering new layers of implications with each round.

* It is good to have a concise and unobstructive "mantra" to touch at periodic moments in your learning that can quickly bring you back into an alpha state. On the first page of the *Mishnah Brura* (a code of Jewish law) is a highly recommended Jewish meditation that is perfect for this practice. Watch your breathing; it should stay slow and deep.

* Note any places where resistance and anxiety appear. Breathe into them. Affirm your commitment to truth:

(I seek truth from the depth of my being. I do not want to be limited by my own narrow-minded conception of what it should look like. I will open myself to these teachings with one condition: Whatever is true should enter my life and take root. Whatever is false should pass through and leave no impression. I trust that it will be so. I embrace truth and deflect falsehood. (A Still Small Voice, Prayer and Destiny, Lesson 1)

✳

Mindy Ribner leads meditation groups regularly in New York City, including her own ongoing group called the Jewish Meditation Circle. Her teaching gives an overview of meditation, with an emphasis on the need to include the personal and the intimate in all parts of our practice. She teaches that if we have a connection with God during our meditation but then are nasty the rest of the day, our meditation work must be improved.

---

5   Keeping God Before Me Always

MINDY RIBNER

In recent years, popular and professional publications have advocated meditation's psychological and physical benefits. Meditation can lower blood pressure, strengthen the immune system, and reduce stress and anxiety. Meditation, along with particular visual imagery, has even been reputed to heal serious physical illnesses, free people of addictive behaviors, and help them gain greater self-mastery. But meditation is more than a stress reducer. It is the vehicle all religions use to impart the esoteric knowledge of their own mystical tradition.

Unfortunately, many Jews seeking the benefits of meditation continue to look outside Judaism for them. They often find themselves practicing other religions, even though that was not their original intention in pursuing meditation. Several months ago, I met a Jewish woman who had practiced Buddhism in

Nepal for over 25 years. She now teaches it. She confided that if she had had access to Kabbalah and Jewish meditation, she would have preferred to stay closer to home. She represents thousands and thousands of people who travel to far, remote places, chanting in foreign languages to foreign gods, even though they may never feel totally comfortable doing so. So hungry are they for spiritual experience and knowledge that they feel they have no other alternative. Jewish meditation may be a door into Judaism for many of these people.

JUDAISM'S MEDITATIVE TRADITIONS

Many people are unaware that there is a mystical and meditative tradition in Judaism. Since meditation and Kabbalah are not yet in the curriculum of most rabbinical seminaries, most rabbis do not have the knowledge to teach or even speak about meditation in their synagogues.

Only in the last fifteen years has the existence of Jewish meditation reached the English-speaking public, primarily through the books of Rabbi Aryeh Kaplan. Rabbi Kaplan, partially motivated by the great interest in Eastern meditation among young Jews, hoped to demonstrate that Judaism had the resources to meet a Jew's spiritual needs. This was a new message for many people who did not consider Judaism or the Jewish community interested in spirituality. Baby boomers grew up in synagogues and Hebrew schools that were not exactly bastions of love and spirituality. Consequently, many Jews chose not to affiliate with Judaism after their bar or bat mitzvah. Others chose not to affiliate with Judaism at all, since, after the Holocaust, many people questioned the efficacy of any identification and involvement with Judaism. It seemed safe to be just "Americans."

I know Americans whose Jewish identity had been kept a secret from them in their youth. It seems to have taken the Jewish community fifty years—two generations after the Holocaust—to begin to heal spiritually and religiously from the Nazi trauma.

Today, more people look toward Judaism for tools to cope with modern life. There is a great interest in Kabbalah and spirituality. Many people believe that we are living at the dawn of a new era of spiritual potential, just as the biblical prophecy predicted: "There will come a time when there will be a hunger and thirst in the land, but the hunger will not be for bread, and the thirst will not be for water, but to hear the word of God." No spiritual practice is as devoted to listening as meditation.

Meditation is the highest path and practice in Judaism. Through it, many of our sages reached their spiritual heights. A person cannot taste the holiness of God, the holiness of their own soul—or the joy of doing a *mitzvah*—without meditation. Contemplative practice is integral to all aspects of Jewish life, since meditation can help focus our energy as we perform a holy act with proper intention. But meditation is more than harnessing *kavvanah* (intention) for the performance of Jewish practice. It is a separate and holy practice and discipline in its own right. Like all forms of Jewish practice, meditation not only refines the practitioner but also brings godliness to the world and reveals the godliness that is already there.

A POTENT TOOL

It has been my great privilege and joy to teach Jewish meditation since 1984 and meditative Kabbalah since 1990. After receiving a nonrabbinical ordination to teach Jewish meditation from the legendary Rabbi Shlomo Carlebach of blessed memory,

I founded the Jewish Meditation Circle, which offers weekly classes in Jewish meditation and meditative Kabbalah. As director of the Circle, I also teach meditation at synagogues of all affiliations throughout the United States and Canada. I have seen that adding even a little meditation to a traditional synagogue service is very potent.

The most dramatic example of this occurred several years ago. I was contacted by a rabbi from Maryland who wanted to learn meditation. He traveled a great distance to see me and, after a few individual sessions with me, invited me to lead a weekend workshop at his synagogue. When I led a guided meditation during his traditional Saturday morning service, the entire prayer service was quickly transformed. I felt that the early sages who wrote the prayer service would have been pleased to see such concentration, such silence, such heartfelt prayers. The rabbi was also amazed and later discovered that seventy-five percent of his congregation was practicing transcendental meditation. These people knew how to meditate but not how to connect meditation with Judaism. Once this connection was made, their Jewish lives were transformed.

As a teacher, I have found that people seek Jewish meditation for a variety of reasons. The most common are stress reduction, personal exploration, and to connect with Jewish spirituality and Jewish practice. Students in my beginning classes are Reform, Conservative, Orthodox, Hasidic, unaffiliated, agnostic, or atheist. Many are not comfortable attending a synagogue service. In a time of increasing polarity in the Jewish community, it is beautiful to see everyone sit together in meditation and experience spiritual intimacy and unity with each other and with the Jewish people as a whole. This suggests that meditation can promote unity among the Jewish people, that Jews who cannot pray together because of ideology can still meditate together.

In its initial stages, Jewish meditation quiets the judgments, fears, doubts, and limiting ideas of the ego mind. Instead, the mind enters ascending levels of focused awareness and filters out spurious thoughts. By lessening the attachment to the physical and extrinsic aspects of self, we become aware of experience and identify with the spiritual and intrinsic true-self. In meditation, we contact and heighten the deep desire within our souls to draw close to the Creator. God responds to the intentions of our heart. As Rabbi Isaac, a great Kabbalist of the twelfth century, said, "As much as the calf wants to suck, the cow wants to give suck." Or, the greater the yearning, the greater the spiritual opening and the greater the spiritual experience.

GOD IS CENTRAL TO MEDITATION

Jewish meditation, through visualization, chanting, and contemplation, facilitates directly experiencing the Divine. Jewish meditation is powerful, transformational, awesome, ecstatic, real, holy. Many people are amazed that such an experience is so readily available to them, that they can glimpse a truly spiritual reality and taste the World to Come.

Unlike Buddhist meditation, God is central to Jewish meditation. This may be problematic for those educated and living in our Western culture, who are confused about who or what God is and ambivalent about the kind of relationship we can have with the Divine. For many people, the word *God* triggers many unresolved feelings. They are more comfortable with words such as *Higher Power, Universal Mind,* or *Cosmic Energy.*

The beginning meditation classes that I teach provide a

laboratory to explore personal spiritual questions as well as begin to heal and transform negative emotions and ideas about self and God. Meditators are not required to hold certain beliefs, but the willingness to be open to what occurs within and to be as honest as possible about it is helpful. As one student said, "For years, I felt strongly about being a Jew in an ethnic way, but I was not open to religion. Through meditation, I found a way to explore my feelings about Judaism. This is the first context in which I have been able to do that without feeling that I should believe something. I find myself offering more faith."

In the beginning classes, the student is guided to both understand and experience the transcendence as well as the immanence of the Creator. In the process, students learn to diminish their self-absorption and become a vessel for the Divine. Students also learn to ask God for what they need.

A DOORWAY TO JUDAISM

Most students are amazed to find that Judaism is sweet, profound, and practical. Unfortunately, most Jews have been restricted to reading the English translations of the Bible without commentary. In these texts, God seems so angry and so jealous that it is understandable that many suspend their involvement with a tradition they believe promulgates a negative concept of God. As the great Rabbi Levy Yitzchok of Berditchev said to a self-proclaimed atheist, "I don't believe in the same God that you don't believe in."

The meditative Kabbalah classes I teach are generally for students who have completed beginning Jewish meditation and want to deepen their experiences. The goal of these classes is to transcend the needs and desires of the ego and align oneself with the Divine will. These meditations begin with a centering and focusing, such as this intention that Kabbalists recommended be said before every prayer or *mitzvah:* "For the sake of the union of the Holy One, Blessed be He and the *Shechinah,* to unite the Name *yod heh* with *vav heh* in a perfect union in the name of all Israel." We spiritually connect ourselves with the Jewish people as a whole, feeling ourselves to be historically part of a chain, riding on the spiritual benefits our predecessors so lovingly bequeathed to us. We attach ourselves to the Jewish people as a whole and to other groups of people who are devoted to the spiritual work of bringing godliness into this physical world. We feel ourselves as a link in this holy chain. We give and receive spiritual support from this connection.

In some meditations, we may journey through spiritual worlds and through *sefirot.* We visualize letters of the Divine Name inside the body, outside the body, and in the various spiritual worlds. We make unification between the various names of God. We meditate on Hebrew letters and how they form words. A single meditation session is usually an hour and a half and is extremely powerful and often ecstatic.

Though meditation is most powerful in a group, meditators need to develop a daily practice. Meditation must be integrated into a person's being and life, or it is simply a fleeting intoxication with no lasting value. The purpose of Jewish meditation is not just to produce glorious spiritual experiences, but also to help us discover who we really are and fulfill our life purpose: to be more truly ourselves, to express our divine potential, and to contribute to bringing and revealing godliness in this world in the unique ways that each of us can. Reb Zusya, an enlightened and beloved mystic of the eighteenth century, said, "When I die, I will be asked by the heavenly Court not why was I not Moses, but why was I not Zusya?" The goal in your life is to be the best *you*. No one else can do that for you.

At a certain point, my students ask how they can best incorporate Jewish meditation into their daily life. I may suggest that beginning students do specific breathing techniques and then focus on a verse of *Tehillim* (Psalms) or a Hebrew mantra. I suggest that they take time to mentally connect and talk to God. In the beginning, meditating at home for five to ten minutes in the morning and evening is fine. I have also developed instructional tapes for students to use in their meditation practice at home.

As students build their spiritual discipline, they begin to understand the power of daily prayer and meditation. Jews are obligated to pray every day, since prayer is so nurturing. Yet, I know that many people have difficulty accessing the prayer book and feel stifled by the rote nature of traditional prayers. I have felt this myself at times. But I am fortunate that when I have difficulty praying, I can meditate to connect to God. Traditional prayer is not my only way to connect with God, and it should not be anyone else's sole way, either. Generally speaking, however, if you progress in meditation, you can pray with *kavvanah* (concentration) and understand the deeper meaning of the words of the prayer. In my classes, students learn certain additional *kavvanot* to include in the traditional prayers. As the words of the prayers become more familiar, the prayers themselves become like a long mantra.

Prayer and meditation go together like the inhalation and exhalation of the breath. A good meditation is often sandwiched between words of prayer, just as heartfelt prayer is preceded and followed by meditation. Rabbi Carlebach described the distinction between prayer and meditation beautifully and succinctly:

"Prayer is the time when I speak to God as the Creator of the world. Meditation is when it is clear to me that God is my closest friend, that God is even closer to me than my own breath."

For example, in a preparatory meditation to prayer, we quiet the chatter of the mind and relax the body. We then reflect on what we really want to receive from God and open our heart and soul to let God be present for us. We reflect on whether what we want is consistent with what we imagine God wants from us. In meditation, we become aware of the presence of God. We reflect on how God is the Creator of everything and everyone and that there is truly no place where He is not. As the Psalms say, "The whole world is full of His Glory." God is where we are. This preparatory experience lets us be wholehearted while speaking directly to God. When prayer is said with this kind of *kavvanah*, we can be lifted up to a place beyond words, a place where we experience intimacy with the Creator. At such a moment, we intuitively understand the words of the Psalm, "Silence is praise." Eventually, however, the mind and heart begin to conceptualize this experience with words of praise and gratitude, and we enter a more prayerful awareness. I often conclude prayer and meditation with reflections about how to bring this heightened God awareness into daily life.

BRINGING MEDITATION
INTO OUR LIVES

One way that a Jew brings God into daily physical life is through *mitzvot*. *Mitzvot* help elevate and sanctify the more mundane aspects of life, and meditation deepens the experience and the power of doing a *mitzvah*. For example, when we say a blessing, "*Baruch atah Adonai,*" "Blessed are You, Lord," we open to the experience of direct connection to the Divine. If we meditate on each word of the blessing, and particularly on the letters of the Divine Name, we become a vessel to receive spiritual energy drawn down by the blessing.

Because meditation helps people recognize that their well-being is directly related to their connection to God, they seek additional ways to connect with God in their daily life. They attend synagogue on Shabbat and holidays. They pray and meditate daily. They practice affirmations. They take moments during the day to center themselves through meditation and God awareness. They begin reading Jewish philosophy or attend classes on Judaism. Many learn Hebrew because they want to pray from the prayer book with a congregation or at home.

For many of my students, the doors into Judaism would not have been opened if not for Jewish meditation and kabbalistic teaching. For many people like myself, meditation is absolutely essential. As Rav Kook said in *The Lights of Holiness*, "Whoever feels within himself, after many trials, that his inner being can find peace only in the secret teachings of the Torah, must know with certainty that it is for this he was created."

Meditation can transform our lives. Whether we are doing a meditation sitting, walking on the street, washing dishes, or with friends, we can easily tune into our breath and become aware of God's Presence and Love in the moment. As King David says, "I have placed the Infinite One before me at all times." This is the goal of meditation. A father once brought his ten-year-old daughter to a class I was teaching. As she was leaving, I asked her what she had learned or experienced during the meditation. She innocently and succinctly summed up the purpose and essence of Jewish meditation: "Before, I thought that God was just in the synagogue. Now I know that God is with me at all times." Wherever we are, in every moment, we can remember that we are in the Divine Presence. This is our joy and our challenge.

✴

Jonathan Omer-Man is the founder and director of Metivta, a school of Jewish wisdom and meditation in Los Angeles. In this teaching, he is concerned with meditation as a steady practice, without frills or false ecstasy.

---

6   Noble Boredom: How to View Meditation

RABBI JONATHAN OMER-MAN

The English writer C. Day Lewis once said that the reason he prayed was because he had to. For some people, the contemplative life is an absolute necessity. You can assuage the need for going to the movies by smoking dope or by getting involved in a thousand and one other endeavors. But at a certain point, the point when you discover the contemplative path, it is clearly your path. Contemplative practice is a method of discovering one's path and how to progress along it and how to be less consumed by diversions and distraction.

Ultimately, a contemplative life is a way of being in the world. For those who have this predisposition, it is extremely valuable. It isn't a way for everybody. It's very important to acknowledge that, for most people, the contemplative is irrelevant. For some people, it is more important than anything else.

Contemplative practice is not like an addiction, though. It is an innate path. It isn't just that persons must find what their soul needs, but almost as if there are different kinds of souls and each proceeds along different kinds of paths: *This* is the path for my kind of soul. This is the way my life unfolds. This is the way that, whatever my task is in this world, it is more likely to be fulfilled.

One of the problems of our time is the excessive development of the sense of the individual. This really has nothing to do with a sense of path, but more the sense of striving and of expansion. The distinction between them is the same distinction between creating and discovery. Discovery is uncovering what is already there. But creating is building something that was never there. One example in music would be Bach, who discovered patterns that were there, whereas romantics are people who create things that were never there.

A few years ago, I had dinner with some friends who were scientists at Cal-Tech. One of them talked about the Galileo Space Program, which sent space probes twice around the moon and the earth, then to Mars and beyond. The phrase used about the people working on it was that they had "discovered" the trajectory of the outgoing orbits. For me, this was an incredible validation of discovery of uncovering hidden patterns. Someone who contemplates is a discoverer. The ecstatic is a creator.

AVOID BECOMING ADDICTED TO THE "HIGHS"

I look at meditation fairly narrowly. Ultimately, it is a daily practice that is boring and that is transformative and doesn't necessarily offer you incredible experiences. The "highs" are not the goal. When we are twenty, we define a relationship by the intensity of the orgasm. Then you get a little bit of life in you and realize that marrying someone because of the intensity of orgasm is really very naive. And one doesn't always even marry the person with whom one has the best sex. Such things are incredible gifts, and we wouldn't want to think about life without them. But they are simply a high.

For many years, I wanted to be an ecstatic. Then, I regarded myself as a failed ecstatic. I could never do what my Sufi friends could do or what my ecstatic Jewish friends could do. Finally, I realized that ecstasy wasn't really a central part of my path. And that I could do pretty well without it.

The ecstatic is a person who has transformative moments of very high intensity. It is relatively easy to bring someone to ecstasy. But what do you do afterwards? The contemplative path is slower and steadier and concentrates more on ongoing awareness than these very intense flashes. Contemplatives have had ecstatic moments, and ecstatics, I assume, have contemplative periods. But we must beware of an addiction for the high. This is especially true in American society because Americans worship high events.

Ultimately, the contemplative knows that life is boring. Aristotle distinguished between noble boredom and ignoble/base boredom. It is very important that we cultivate a sense of noble boredom, of being without the need for action, without the need for something to happen.

Noble boredom means no anticipation of action. It means having the ability to be present without needing something to happen. This is one of the most important things in meditative practice. I have a great suspicion of pyrotechnics and explosive sparks. Seeking these is not really meditation. They may have value and their place, but they are not really meditation. To illustrate this, I would like to draw on the image of marriage. A good marriage is when the two partners know that there is an element of boredom with which they must live. They ultimately accept the richness of the boredom. This allows for occasional high peaks. But the need for more excitement is dangerous and a diversion from the essence of the practice.

I question whether meditation can be fit into mainstream Jewish practice because it's ultimately a minority practice. In synagogues, a rabbi will start doing meditation, and half the people there don't want it, perhaps a quarter do, and the rest are curious. Meditation is not a "main sanctuary" activity. It is not something to be added to services precisely because many people don't want or understand it.

I don't know how this will be worked out. There is a problem of size, which is very significant in contemporary American Judaism. We need large institutions to pay rabbis, to have dayschools and afternoon schools, and to have educators. A group of fifty meditators are not going to be able to build a school for their kids or to maintain Jewish services. They cannot even maintain a building. So one of the tragedies of the modern temple is that it has become a coalition of many different needs and often sinks to the lowest common denominator.

For a small percentage of people, meditating is the most natural thing in the world. They move directly into it. For most of us, it's a struggle. This is why the group is important: it reinforces our desire to meditate. In many ways, learning to meditate is changing the way we use our minds. Of course, there are profoundly different kinds of meditation, but common to each is observing how the mind works.

THE VALUE OF BOREDOM

There are many models of mind in various civilizations. Plato defined the mind as a rider of a chariot with two horses, one white and one dark. Spiritually, understanding the mind is a way of promoting and deepening one's spiritual work and understanding the nature of one's path. It is a true understanding of the unfolding of our life.

There is no easy way to integrate this. A practice like Shabbat is very helpful, since this one day can affect the rest of your life. Sitting in meditation for twenty minutes every morning is the same. But it's a slow process and can take months or years.

For many people, the main difficulty of meditating is that it's scary to open the closets of the mind. You don't know exactly where you're going and you don't know whether it is worthwhile. But if you belong to a meditation group, you can discover these difficulties with others and realize that they are remarkably banal and ordinary and that everybody has them. My own meditation has led me to a certain amount of equanimity and helped me to become a more responsive and a less reactive person. Not a less spontaneous person, but a less automatically reactive person.

Another common obstacle to practice is how to carry on in a dry period. How do you have the momentum to carry through when nothing happens? Then one must seek external reinforcements, such as group practice.

Another difficulty is loss of meaning. At a certain point during their meditation career, everyone thinks, "Why am I bothering with this?" Then you must rediscover meaning. An aspect of difficulty is the difficulty itself. The chatter and the reactiveness of the mind are all-pervading. But one thing I've always found with meditation is that the difficulties are the major part of the course.

You must make the leap forward from difficulty, and this can't be done with ease. The obstacles themselves are points of transformation. This is a very hard truth.

Another aspect of this is that one component of a spiritual practice is becoming a better person. This is true transformation of self, but it is very hard. It is similar to the difference between turning around a 250,000-ton tanker or a rowboat. A rowboat can be turned around in a moment, but a tanker takes three days. We are much like this. Patience is key.

So, an example: A particular politician makes us angry. He might be a self-righteous liar. A spiritual practice demands that we be alert to when we ourselves are being drawn into an inner drama of anger or fear and so on. As we observe it, we become more truly responsive and less reactive. A red flag comes up in the mind, as it were, denoting an obsessive reaction. From this, I learn to budget my energies more effectively and pay far less attention to this politician.

THE REWARDS OF DISCIPLINE

My own spiritual practice became more formalized when I was in my midthirties because that was when I found some meditation teachers. In my forties, it became integrated into a Jewish practice. I have a strong regular practice, but there are times when it just disappears. I understand the disappearing within the context of the whole of the practice. It isn't that I have a practice—and then I don't have a practice, but rather that my practice includes periods in which I lose my practice. For me,

this is an important distinction. It isn't that I have a relationship with the Divine that I sometimes lose. But sometimes my
relationship includes periods of profound doubt, or my practice is boring. It's just sitting, yet it's an incredibly rich part of
my life. I feel it has changed my path in the world and is something I very much want to share with other people.

Part of my life's work is to make Judaism more hospitable
to people like me. This is, I think, occurring. But there are dangers, as well. For example, a number of people who can't
meditate are actually teaching meditation. This is very disturbing. Very often, these folks who can't meditate teach kabbalistic
meditations that induce a high. Another concern is what I call
"medicalized meditation." People who offer this strip meditation of its spiritual components and say, "Do this; it will make
you feel better. It will reduce your anxiety, and your blood pressure will drop twenty points." But the spiritual component is
the doorway to true transformation. Without it, progress cannot be achieved.

Ultimately, enjoy your successes, but do not get too excited
by them. Just keep plugging away.

✳

Avram Davis is the founder of Chochmat HaLev, a school and practice center for Jewish meditation in Berkeley, California. He is the
author of *The Way of the Flame: A Guide to the Forgotten Mystical
Tradition of Jewish Meditation* (HarperCollins). In this teaching, he
is concerned with the way Jewish meditation is shaping itself in contemporary society and some of the basic obstacles to meditation
practice.

---

7 Jewish Meditation Today and Its Obstacles

AVRAM DAVIS

Three "schools" of meditation appear to be now solidifying
within Judaism. Different teachers call them by different names,
but the basic teachings are quite similar, whether the teacher is
in Israel, Europe, Australia, or the United States. These are *ayin*
meditation, *chesed* meditation, and kabbalistic meditation.

Gershom Scholem, a twentieth-century scholar, felt that the
early Kabbalists did not differentiate between meditation and
contemplation,[1] but this insight should be extended. Both the
early Kabbalists and indeed the *Tannaim* (first generations of
talmudic writers) and *Amoraim* (second generations of talmudic
writers) referred constantly to *tefillah*, a word usually translated
as "prayer," in a very ambiguous way. These early teachers did
not clearly distinguish between what we call prayer and what

we today call simple meditation. They tended to move back and forth between these spiritual methods or modes very quickly. When they use the term *tefillah*, they can easily be referring to either meditation or prayer or possibly to both. It is both a strength and a weakness of modernity that we feel so sharply the need to differentiate between these transformative tools. Deep meditation was certainly practiced by the early Kabbalists, but additional barriers to its widespread use were erected by the rabbis who feared its disruptive effects. I believe these fears were perhaps well founded for their historical moment but are not valid today. The general sophistication of modern Americans and Israelis, coupled with a thirst for spiritual transformation, creates an ideal situation for the deepening of Jewish spirituality.

Saying this helps us view more easily the place that meditation and deep transformative contemplative work have held in Jewish consciousness for at least four millennia. Yet, many of our early teachers perceived deep contemplative work as potentially dangerous. Consequently, it seems to have been relegated to (and regulated by) a relatively tiny number of adherents. This circle was greatly widened with the reformation of the Baal Shem Tov, the founder of Hasidism and his disciples in the early 1700s. But the political and social pressure of living under the oppression of a hostile majority culture forced many of his reformations to subside and be taken over again by an elite group.

Another factor was the Holocaust. The utter obliteration of schools and lineages hindered the dissemination of teaching. It also made many of the surviving teachers more conservative in their transmission. We are now, though, in a period of great rediscovery, transition, and translation—a period of re-idiomizing this great treasure of Jewish spirituality—the meditative tradition.

The three forms of Jewish meditation—*ayin, chesed* and

kabbalistic—have, of course, many subsets and crossovers. Many teachers draw from more than one of these forms. But all of the teachings I know fall broadly into one of these three types.

AYIN MEDITATION

Ayin literally means "nothingness" or "the void." It derives ultimately from the first principle of the Torah path, which is that God is One. *Ayin* is the state of complete Oneness, by which is meant either God or the egoless state of a person who is in complete unity with God. The active form of this cleaving is often called *devekut*, literally "merging" or "cleaving." Both Kabbalists and modern scholars have long recognized that there are several stages of *ayin*, or *devekut*. As Scholem wrote, "...there [are] different ranks of *devekut* itself, such as 'equanimity'; *hishtavvut*...'solitude'; *Hitbodedut*, 'holy spirit' and 'prophecy'."[2] *Ayin* is a state of Essence. It is the Ground of Being. It is God itself. One may think of it as the quality of soul that is beyond time, space, or any corporeality. Each person may access this place. In the truest sense, each person *is* this. But it is unrecognized and unknown in most people's lives. A meditation I use often in my teaching is derived from Dov Baer of Mezritch. Dov Baer teaches extensively about *ayin* in his book *Maggid D'v'rav l'Yakov*. The bulk of his teaching helps us to first perceive *ayin* as an "in-between" space. One homey example he gives of an in-between space is when an egg becomes a chicken. It is the space that occurs after words are dropped away and before the next word appears. It is spacious and without boundary. It is nothingness, but it is also Godness. It is the most profound of spaces. I direct my meditators to concentrate on this in-between place, allowing them to begin to experience *ayin*.

CHESED MEDITATION

Chesed is loving-kindness. It is both journey and destination. One of the most straightforward ways in which *ayin* can be experienced is through *chesed*. Some of our teachers of blessed memory insisted that awe or fear is another absolute element of *ayin* apprehension, but it seems to me that the preponderance of the tradition points toward *chesed* and its various permutations such as mercy, charity, and compassion as being the very fabric of the universe. Bachya ben Asher, a scholar of the thirteenth century who synthesized the flowering of Spanish Jewish philosophy, wrote that a love of the Divine is "an obligatory commandment constituting a principal cornerstone for...fulfillment of the Torah."[3] An early kabbalistic text, the *Reshit Chochma,* reiterates this even more forcefully: "When a man denies the obligation to loving kindness, it is as though he had denied the Root [of Being]."[4]

KABBALAH MEDITATION

Kabbalah is the most mental of the "schools." Using mind to break mind, it often relies on fierce study, complicated visualizations of God's names, and recitations of the letters and names of Power to break through the veil of ego.

WHY WE MEDITATE

All meditation practice is predicated on two principles of "why": all people start and sustain their meditation practice either because they have experienced the sweetness of God—a unifying experience, a moment of *devekut*—and want more of this experience or because they have experienced the sharp angst of existence—the pain of loss, the fear of death, the despair of failure and destruction—and they want less. This is what the Torah defines as the "curse."

In this sense, we are all simple creatures, and we were meant to be so. We want less pain and more joy. Ultimately, all practice derives from this. We pursue a spiritual discipline precisely because of a promised payoff: greater peace, greater equanimity, greater joy *or* less pain, less depression.

Consequently, everyone is suited for meditation—sometimes. Meditation has the ability to deepen our knowledge of ourselves very quickly. By doing this, it permits soul, or essence, to emerge. This itself can create a difficulty. Chief among these is the *level* of self-inquiry; that is, just how "deep" does one want to go? The old joke "You're giving me more information than I want to know" certainly can hold true here. There are moments in our life when we don't *want* transformation. Or, if we do, we want damn little. So, there is the matter of limits and progressing at our own speed. There is no ultimate hurry in this business. Since we're stuck with ourselves, we need to work with ourselves in a comfortable way.

HOW TO BEGIN

Saying this, though, reiterates the power of meditation to give us insight. But meditation is not brain surgery. We should just start—from wherever we are. Once, for instance, a student came to a master and asked how she could approach God. He told her to be quiet and after a moment said, "What do you hear?"

"Nothing," she replied.

"Start from there," he said.

Wherever we are is the most important first step. Keep remembering that at every moment of every day, we are at whatever place we find ourselves. We must reevaluate and reexamine our road. Otherwise, the entire endeavor becomes rote and stale.

My teacher used to say that to have the opportunity to give a thirsty person a glass of water provides enough joy to dance for seventy years!

OBSTACLES TO PRACTICE

Every moment, we start again. This is the nature of God's joy. It is ever fresh. Sometimes it seems as if this joy is difficult to access. Our lives are busy and complicated. And we have fear: fear of discovering and fear of losing our fear. But fear, depression, and laziness are all part of us. How can they be dispelled? There are two broad manners, both of which have support within the tradition. The first is to hammer the darkness, to actually wrestle and fight with the various obstacles of our mind. The second way insists that darkness is also part of the light and that the only way, ultimately, of dispelling darkness is by introducing more light. With more light, the shadows are dispersed and then are simply gone, absorbed as it were into the light. Both are holy ways, but as a teacher I tend to follow the latter, which I believe is the path most true to the deepest intent of the tradition.

✳

Dr. Alan Brill is an Orthodox rabbi and professor at Yeshiva University in New York. Besides teaching classes on Jewish mysticism, he conducts small groups in meditation. In this teaching, Brill situates meditation in the larger stream of Jewish thought and presents some of the different types of meditation discussed by the tradition.

---

8   The Hierarchy of Jewish Meditation

RABBI ALAN BRILL

Jewish spirituality encompasses a wide variety of experiences generally associated with meditation. Traditional Jewish texts expect the pious to visualize God's name continuously, to constantly sense God's providence; to be committed to daily or weekly sessions of self-scrutiny and outpouring of the heart to God, and to sense the inner meaning of the Sabbath and holidays.

In contrast, the Jewish meditation that I will discuss here is a hierarchical ladder of internal states. It provides in its earliest stages a tether to calm the emotions. This helps enhance intention in the ordinary practice of prayer and in continuously focusing on God' s presence. In its higher stages, it leads to equanimity, freedom from negative emotions, better control over the mind, and added creativity and gives a sense of the Divine energies present in prayer, study, and performing the commandments. It also deals with creativity, pain, sickness, and trauma.

All this gives a sense of well-being, wholeness, balance, and compassion. The highest levels are those that channel the flow of the Divine and prophetic inspiration from their supernal dwellings into the mundane world.

Most medieval religious commentators, such as Maimonides, Nachmanides, and the students of Rabbi Yonah of Gerona, assume that we need meditative intention in prayer. These are not isolated opinions but are the codified legal requirements for prayer found in the *Tur*, the fifteenth-century codification of Jewish law. Therefore, one of the first goals of a Jewish meditative practice is to be conscious of God's glory when you pray.

ASCENDING TO THE DIVINE

The Zohar, Rabbi Moses de Leon, and Rabbi Joseph Gikkatila all have meditations on Divine lights and names that help us ascend into the higher realms of divinity. A lower level of divinity is immanent and embodied in this world and receives its light from above. This is similar to light shining into a prism. But there is a higher realm of light that is God's manifestation and power. Finally, there is an infinite realm of brilliant shining light that is the source of all light, energy, and power. You can slowly ascend to the infinite realm by climbing this heavenly ladder. To work successfully with this map, you work on giving it clarity and depth and creating secure mental safety nets. Then you can bind yourself with emotion, will, and intellect to the light, and it will bind its infinite emotion, will, and intellect to you. As you slowly descend, you bring the infinite light into this world, letting it grow and giving it energy. Then it cascades into your mind, and visualization of the Divine Name permeates your body and the room where you sit. You have made sure that it is channeled slowly and safely to avoid being over-whelmed.

Medieval Kabbalists used this meditation during prayer so they could ascend to the infinite realm before the silent *Amidah* (the silent standing prayer) during worship. Variants of this meditation use a candle flame, different colored lights, Divine names, or the parts or levels of the soul (like *nefesh*, *ruach*, *chayah*, and *neshamah*). Each provides an element of psychic development that parallels the gradual development of God's manifestation.

Maimonides presents a non-visual path for entering this hierarchy in his *Mishneh Torah*. He considers this the path to prophecy. Before embarking upon it, you should have deep knowledge, moral virtues, and near control of your desires. Then you can contemplate the higher realms and train your mind to focus on the Divine at all times. This is a transformative proc-ess in which the practitioner can become holy and angelic. In *The Guide to the Perplexed*, Maimonides shows that it applies to anyone who wishes to truly serve God.

LEARNING THE BASICS

The initial sessions in meditation classes emphasize the basic skills needed to succeed. The first class is about how to sit prop-erly, relax the body, and slow down our busy minds, since we all need to learn how to tether our minds and focus them. Es-sential for meditation is learning how to let go of distractions and let them flow away gently. I explain how emotions that dis-tract us during meditation need to be confronted and worked through slowly. Only then can we let go of their hurt.

The next step during classes is to try various Jewish meditative techniques and develop a conceptual framework for using them. We do a simplified version of an ascent from *The Gate of Intention* (authorship uncertain, traditionally attributed to the school of Azriel of Gerona) and practice light meditations from the Zohar. These meditations increase our ability to develop a space in the mind for visualizing the Divine Name. Eventually, we progress to meditations on the *Ein Sof*, which is literally the "Without End" and refers to that aspect of divinity that is beyond conceptualization.

We discuss colors, shapes, lights, bringing Divine energy down, and how to avoid distracting images. And we reorient ourselves from the popular modern image of God as an old man with a white beard to a Jewish view of God as the source of energy and as a hierarchy of divinity.

EMPTYING OUR MINDS

Next, I introduce students to Hasidic techniques that help us sense the divinity immanent in the world. Stillness, emptying the mind, and selflessness quiet the mind further and open us to the world around us. Infusing routine acts of everyday life, such as eating and drinking, with worshipful intention allows the sense of the Divine gained in the ascent meditations to be embodied in this world.

Finally, we attempt to practice some basic techniques found in kabbalistic writings. It may take months of practice to reach the level where we can properly meditate using the techniques of Rabbi Isaac Luria, the great medieval Kabbalist of Safed, in which we combine various forms of the Divine Name and use them to channel Divine energy into our lives.

For those students who feel that there is too much emphasis on metaphysics, we finally dissolve the kabbalistic structures by focusing on nothingness. This technique causes the clutter of the mind to fade away, leaving a path directing the meditator to the infinite.

BARRIERS TO MEDITATION

Most Westerners have trouble sitting still and releasing their tension. When I first started teaching meditation to Talmud students who had not come to me to learn how to meditate, I discovered that most of them could not sit still, stop worrying about their busy schedules, or slow down their bodies. Many complained about pain in their back and neck, scrunched their eyes tight, contorted their bodies, or had various psychosomatic ailments. This surprised me because traditional Kabbalists and various Americans and Israelis attracted to meditation can sit quite still. I realized that most of those I met who were meditating were a self-elected group who could focus on one point and led nonpressured lives. So I understood that I had to cull advice from pietistic literature about how to start practicing. My only (conscious) modification of the tradition was to start the first class with everyone relaxing their bodies as is done in a pain reduction class or a birthing class.

There is a story: A sage once came to one of the meditators and asked that he be accepted into their society.

The other replied, "My son, blessed are you to God. Your intentions are good. But tell me, have you attained equanimity or not?"

The sage said, "Master, explain your words."

The meditator said, "If someone is praising you and another is insulting, are the two equal in your eyes or not?"

He replied, "No, my master, I have pleasure from those who praise me and pain from those who degrade me. But I do not take revenge or bear a grudge."

The other said, "Go in peace, my son. You have not attained equanimity. You are not prepared for your thoughts to be bound on high, that you should come and meditate. Go and increase the humbleness of your heart, and learn to treat everything equally until you have become tranquil. Only then will you be able to meditate."

Aryeh Kaplan, who retold this medieval story, produced great introductions to the world of Jewish meditation, but he was negligent in leaving out the basic steps in meditation. A reader of Kaplan's works would enter the meditative realm with too much self-concern and personal desire. Basic steps are needed to let you work on the visualization techniques without the distraction of thoughts and emotions. These basic steps also release tension and emotions to prevent harm from these techniques. You could burn up in self-effacement or self-delusion if you used the advanced techniques in Kaplan's books without adequate preparation.

Another obstacle is knowing your limits so you don't attempt more than you are ready to handle. You also need to practice regularly and integrate meditation into your ordinary religious life. Maimonides suggests starting a meditative practice by focusing on the unity of God during the *Sh'ma* and then, after several years, proceeding to more advanced practices. You have to start slowly and integrate one or two lines of instruction at a time, gradually stabilizing the images and avoiding being distracted by even the most alluring visions. You also need to beware of destructive plunges into an annihilating nothingness.

TURNING OUR WHOLE LIFE
INTO A MEDITATION

Integrating meditation into your daily life involves assessing your schedule and lifestyle and determining how to devote some time each day to meditative practices. Set aside time on Thursday night to review your week and meditate on the coming Sabbath. A meditation on Saturday night can infuse the coming week with Sabbath awareness. A two-hour welcoming of the Sabbath on Friday evening using various meditations and contemplative readings transforms the Sabbath into a time when you can experience a heightened consciousness. Before the holidays, a similar process is needed to sense the presence of that holiday.

Rabbi Zadok HaCohen of Lublin describes religious life as a process of growth along a sliding scale in which we integrate ever greater parts of consciousness toward Divine knowledge and unity. Focused concentration is only one part of attaining continuous consciousness of God. Eventually, our whole life can be directed toward becoming filled with the oneness of the Divine and knowing that God is with us at all times—and we are with God.

✸

Dr. Edward Hoffman practices Kabbalah and clinical psychology in New York City. Well-known for his many books, such as *The Heavenly Ladder* and *The Way of Splendor*, Dr. Hoffman seeks to combine the insights of modern psychology with the traditional wisdom of Jewish mysticism. Here, he considers the relationship between various states of consciousness and meditation.

---

9 Opening the Inner Gates

EDWARD HOFFMAN

The days pass and are gone, and one finds that he never once had time to really think.... One who does not meditate cannot have wisdom.

— *Rabbi Nachman of Breslov*

It is almost a truism to say that we live in a tense and hurried society. After all, our age has been dubbed the "Age of Anxiety," a seemingly inevitable accompaniment to our fast-paced, technological civilization. Millions of people in the United States and other Western nations suffer daily from hypertension and cardiovascular disease, two illnesses that are very related to our way of life. To try coping with stress, many people turn to medication, either prescribed or illicit. Others seek refuge in alcohol or the monotony of evening after evening in front of the television set. Even "surfing the Net" can be addictive. None of these activities, which are all essentially passive, deals directly with the underlying cause of our inner discontents.

Though Eastern spiritual teaching first found voice in America in the 1840s with Emerson and Thoreau, in recent years there has been another tremendous influx of Eastern spiritual teachings. These have brought to public awareness an alternative approach to our emotional well-being. These teachings involve meditation. Not long ago, this ancient practice was usually associated with skinny Hindu ascetics wearing loincloths and turbans. The term itself connoted arcane religious dogmas of a vanished era and seemed to hold little relevance for our own sophisticated time. Moreover, claims made by adherents loomed as extravagant, sometimes almost ludicrous. Even the most patient individuals, Western science assured us, could not possibly learn to control their heartbeat or respiration simply by staring at their navel or a colorful symbol. Outside of a few zealous devotees, there was meager interest in the West in this ancient discipline.

This entire situation has now radically changed. All over the globe, people with minimal background in Eastern philosophies are regularly performing different types of meditation. Dating back to Harvard professor Herbert Benson's *The Relaxation Response* in the 1960s, books elucidating this subject have become bestsellers. Increasingly in scientific and research laboratories, American researchers have clearly demonstrated that each of us is indeed capable of influencing the most subtle aspects of our mental and physical being. Biofeedback research has moved from the fringes of psychology and medicine to the forefront of these fields. A growing body of scientific evidence has shown the efficacy of meditation in health care. Mainstream health maintenance organizations, clinics, and hospitals are now promoting meditation as a viable, often safer and preferable alternative to chemical and surgical interventions. In addition, psychological study of various forms of meditation has yielded valuable insights about how our mind ordinarily functions and, perhaps more significantly, provocative notions about how we can greatly improve our mental capacity by training ourselves to meditate. In the coming years, meditation seems likely to attract greater interest throughout our society.

Nevertheless, to many people, meditation has remained virtually synonymous with the exotic mores of India and Tibet. No doubt this erroneous perception derives from the very real impact that such Eastern religious figures as the Dalai Lama have exerted on the West. However, nearly every culture in recorded history seems to have been familiar with formal methods for enhancing our normal flow of consciousness.

In China, Taoists used altered forms of breathing to modify their mental states. In Siberia, shamans relied on the psychedelic properties of sacred plants as well as extremes of bodily self-punishment to propel themselves into heightened realms of awareness. On our own continent, Native American tribal leaders and healers have made use of fasting and arduous "vision quests" alone in the wilderness to provoke dramatic changes in their experience of the cosmos.

During Judaism's 4,000-year history, it has developed one of the world's most comprehensive meditative traditions. For millennia, the Jewish visionary way has been avidly interested in meditation and what it can offer us in our daily lives. To be sure, Judaism's chief concerns have been the larger Jewish community and the individual's ethical relation to it. Yet Judaism's Kabbalistic side has, for centuries, focused extensively on the nature of our habitual thought-stream and how to transform it through disciplined meditation, prayer, and study. To those who view the study of higher consciousness as lying solely within the province of Hindu yogis or Tibetan lamas, it may be quite a revelation to learn of the Kabbalah's major involvement with this fascinating topic.

BALANCING OUR VARIOUS "SOULS"

From its inception, Kabbalah insisted that our normal waking state is, by its very essence, filled with conflicting thoughts and desires. Kabbalah's leading thinkers stressed that the average person is ceaselessly at odds with himself or herself. "Within each human are all the warring factions," stated Rabbi Nachman of Breslov, a Hasidic rebbe (or spiritual teacher). "His personality is that of the victorious nation. Each time, a different nation is victorious and he must change completely....This can drive him insane." Similarly, in the early eighteenth century, the Italian Kabbalist Rabbi Moses Chaim Luzzatto succinctly commented, "The Highest Wisdom decreed that each person should consist of two opposites...in a constant state of battle."

The Kabbalists regarded this inner unease as basic to the human condition. Indeed, they deemed it to be an essential part of our earthly purpose as individuals and as members of our species. In fact, the Jewish esoteric system argues that we each have been created with several separate, but interrelated levels of consciousness or "souls." Our lowest desires, originating in the *nefesh* (animal soul) and *ruach* (emotional soul), urge us to fulfill our instinctual needs and little else. These innate animalistic drives are, by necessity, very powerful, since they ensure our physical maturation and survival. But, the Kabbalah adds, we are also born with a *neshamah*, a transcendent Self that takes years to rise above our petty, material wants. Moreover, according to some Kabbalists, we also have even more exalted internal aspects. Known as *chayah* and *yechidah*, these lie almost wholly dormant during our day-to-day existence, so tenuous is their connection to the body.

Most of us cannot help but sense the presence within us of vast, unused potentialities. So throughout our lifetime, we experience an ever-present struggle among the different parts of our personality. To the Kabbalists, though, this state of affairs is hardly insoluble. By exerting our conscious willpower, we can learn to overcome the emotional bonds that keep us fettered to trivialities. Though few of us can realistically aspire to have complete power over our anger or depression, we do have far more ability than we think. "Everyone can have absolute control over his thoughts and direct them as he wishes," Rabbi Nachman of Breslov emphatically declared.

Nachman's Hasidic contemporary, Rabbi Schneur Zalman of Liady, likewise observed in the *Tanya* (his magnum opus) that any of us can become at least a *benoni*, an intermediary in status between the lowly "normal" and the true t*zaddik*—one who experiences each moment as filled with supernal radiance. Describing the *benoni*, Rabbi Zalman explained that "the three 'garments' of the animal soul, namely, thought, speech, and act, originating in the *kelipah* [realm of impurity] do not prevail within him over the divine soul." But attaining even this "intermediary" goal can still be very elusive, as the Kabbalists knew. Intimately familiar with the workings of the human mind, they acutely understood the chasm that divides our daily mental condition from more lofty perceptions.

Thus, in language strikingly reminiscent of contemporary philosophy, an anonymous disciple of the thirteenth-century

Kabbalist, Abraham Abulafia, metaphorically lamented, "It is not seemly that a rational being held captive in prison should not search out every means, a hole or a small fissure, of escape."

The Jewish visionary tradition *does* provide a way out of the isolated cell of our anxious mind. For centuries, the Hebrew term used to describe this has been *devekut*, which refers to the inner state of cleaving to the Divine. Its meaning goes far beyond that of simple relaxation or freedom from tension, though certainly it encompasses these qualities too. Rather, *devekut* implies an inner realm in which everyday worries recede in importance, so ecstatic and complete is this higher consciousness. The crucial notion is that by calming the whirl of thoughts that occupy our ordinary mind, we open a door that leads to an exalted awareness of the wonder of the entire cosmos. "If one sanctifies himself...," observed Rabbi Luzzatto, "even one's physical actions come to partake of holiness."

Consequently, the major teachers of Jewish meditation have emphasized that specific mental techniques can enable us to transcend the conflicts we feel inside us. In fact, a key distinguishing feature of Kabbalah is this stress upon our own efforts to uplift our mundane awareness, an approach that has generally differed from mainstream Judaism's greater focus upon communal prayer and activity. From the *Merkavah* (a meditation technique that achieves unity with the godhead by visualizations) or "Chariot" practitioners in the ancient Holy Land to the Hasidim of eighteenth-century Eastern Europe, initiates on this path have accorded the highest respect to private meditation as a direct gateway to the Divine.

The Kabbalists typically utilized a wide variety of methods to accomplish this objective. The precise means have varied considerably according to time and locale—and even the personality of the teacher. Some spiritual masters like Rabbi Nachman of Breslov borrowed freely from several Jewish meditative systems to better serve the needs of their adherents. Thus, his colleague and chief scribe, Rabbi Nathan of Nemirov, informs us that his mentor would look at the "root" of each person's soul and prescribe the specific practice necessary to correct that person's flaws. We are further told that there were practices that Rabbi Nachman prescribed for a person's entire lifetime, whereas in other instances, the rebbe "prescribed a certain practice for a given period of time, and then substituted another routine."

This flexibility about technique reflected the kabbalistic dictum that the particular method of self-development is less significant than our actual attitude and commitment to inner growth. Although Jewish visionaries have felt tremendous reverence for the meditative tools passed down from previous generations, they have never elevated these devices above our personal makeup.

Indeed, such sacred works as the thirteenth-century Zohar, the "Book of Splendor," are quite clear on this point. If we are emotionally unequipped to handle the rigors of rather powerful mental disciplines, then we will reap little benefit from them. In fact, they may even substantially harm us, however sincere our motivation. Referring to advanced methods for altering our consciousness, Rabbi Luzzatto commented, "It is obvious...that it is not appropriate for a commoner to make use of the King's scepter. Regarding this, our sages teach us: One who makes use of the Crown will pass away."

In my own clinical practice over the years, I have witnessed this phenomenon. Men and women were sincerely motivated but too hastily took on advanced kabbalistic meditations—

invariably, without a teacher—and suffered significant mental and even physical problems as a result. What ultimately counts is our willingness to be diligent and patient, and not to expect immediate, dramatic results.

THREE BEGINNING MEDITATIONS

I recommend three specific exercises for those beginning to explore Jewish meditation. While none requires any previous background or knowledge in Judaism's meditative tradition, with daily practice, you will definitely experience a variety of benefits in your daily life.

One point to note: It is best to meditate when you are physically alert and not overly fatigued. The goal of Jewish meditation is to help you achieve a higher state of consciousness. If you find yourself becoming drowsy while meditating, this simply means that your body is tired and that you should meditate at an earlier time of day.

Before starting your meditation, make yourself physically comfortable. Sit in a relaxed position, either sitting in a cross-legged position on the floor or with your back erect on a chair. Make sure you will not be disturbed by any distractions, such as the ringing of a telephone. Press your lips lightly together, and breathe gently through your nostrils. For each of these exercises, read the instructions carefully, and then close your eyes.

Exercise 1: Contacting the *Ein Sof,* the "Infinite"

Visualize yourself soaring upward. As you ascend, you feel a growing sense of lightness and mental clarity. As you soar higher and higher, you become aware of the dazzling sea of Light that shines all around you.

This Light is the *Ein Sof* (the kabbalistic term for the "God-force"), which is filled with boundless, creative strength. At this moment, and at every moment of existence, the *Ein Sof* is creating the entire universe anew in dazzling, cascading energy.

Feel the radiance of the *Ein Sof* as it fills the cosmos and the countless stars and worlds of space. This Light connects them all into one supreme whole. Feel this radiance flowing through you and invigorating you with a marvelous sense of well-being. Know that this Light is now generating creative energy to guide and help you. Indeed, the Light is infinite creativity, the source of All.

Be aware of this brilliant radiance that flows throughout the cosmos and throughout your own being for as long as you wish. When you feel ready, let the Light descend until it merges with your normal being. Rest for a few moments, and then thank the *Ein Sof* for letting you experience its presence so fully. Now, go about your day's activities.

Exercise 2: The *Ein Sof* Is Within You

Begin with the preliminaries described in Exercise 1. When you are physically comfortable, visualize a tiny point of light situated about six inches above your head, roughly where the top of a crown would be located. According to the Kabbalah, this is where the vast energy of the *Ein Sof* connects to our own spiritual being. Now, close your eyes, and visualize this minute point of light becoming more and more dazzling. As it sends forth brilliant beams—first in front of you, and then to your right, to your left, and behind you—feel yourself surrounded by a cascading fountain of light.

Now, as you inhale through your nostrils, draw this radiance into your body. Feel it circulating through all the cells of your body, enhancing your sense of vitality and your emotional and spiritual well-being. Feel it increasing your inner strength and clarity. Let the energy of *Ein Sof* go wherever it is needed—physically, emotionally, or spiritually —so it can heal you within.

Now, with your eyes still gently closed, exhale and sense a bluish-like light traveling through your body and leaving through your feet. As it leaves, it removes any toxins, tensions, and negativities that you may have been harboring, either consciously or unconsciously. Feel yourself becoming wonderfully refreshed and cleansed.

Breathe a few more times, in and out, according to the pattern described above. With each cycle, feel yourself vitally connected to the *Ein Sof* and its unimaginable powerful and creative force. Silently ask the *Ein Sof* to guide you with this energy in any challenge you presently experience.

Now, sense the dazzling beams fade and dissolve until only the tiny point of light above your head remains. Finally, the dot of light winks out of existence in our universe. But know that any time you wish to renew or strengthen your connection to the *Ein Sof* for greater physical, emotional, and spiritual well-being, you can do this exercise. Thank the *Ein Sof* for its help, and go about your day's activities.

Exercise 3: Chanting *Shalom*

Make yourself comfortable, and conduct your usual preliminaries. Your focus will be upon the Hebrew word *shalom*, which means "peace" and "wholeness" and interestingly includes the identical "om" sound that is central to Hindu meditation.

Jewish mysticism softens the power of the "om" by utilizing the "shhhhaaa" sound as a jumping-off point, then returning to our ordinary consciousness by using the "mmmmmmm" sound.

Begin by saying *"shalom"* aloud a few times, gradually elongating its syllables. Now, find a rhythm that feels comfortable, yet empowering, by adjusting the length of the "shhhhaaa," "lo," and "mmmmmm" sounds to your preference. They do not have to be of equal length; each can have varying durations.

Historically, Kabbalists have viewed this intriguing phrase as referring to specific methods of meditation such as this.

When you have finished the exercise, thank the *Ein Sof* for permitting you to experience more closely the vast, supernal realm of *shalom* that exists beyond our ordinary frame of awareness.

JOURNALING YOUR MEDITATION

Many people record their meditative experiences in a journal. In my teaching experience, it is especially useful to write down immediately after each session whatever thoughts, images, or feelings came to you. Although you may quickly reap significant benefits in your daily life by daily meditative practice, do not expect overnight change. As Rabbi Nachman of Breslov aptly observed nearly two hundred years ago, "You think that everything comes at once. This is far from the truth. You must work...before you can achieve any good quality."

With the proper attitude of reverence for the holiness of our inner world, you are sure to find Jewish meditation extremely empowering. As the Midrash encouragingly remarks, "The gates are open at every hour, and all who wish to enter, may enter."

✳

David Zeller is an Orthodox rabbi, teacher, and executive director of Yakar Institute, a center of Jewish textual learning and meditation, in Jerusalem. He is grounded in the four-worlds approach, which seeks to perceive reality in multiple ways. Zeller tries to bring the Divine into ordinary day-to-day practice, and his methods combine single-pointedness and transformation.

---

10 A Splendid Way to Live

RABBI DAVID ZELLER

The revelation at Mount Sinai, by all accounts, was an inconceivably incredible experience. It was not a lecture on the theory and practice of Judaism. It was an experience, and not just the experience of one "enlightened" master, but the experience of each and every individual who was at Sinai, each in their own way, differing only in accordance with their own personal level of receptivity.

According to tradition, the revelation lay in God's "speaking" the Ten Commandments, either with an outer voice or an inner voice. Some say it was just the first three of the commandments that were heard. Some say it was just the first commandment, *Anochi haShem*, "I am the Lord your God," that was "heard" by all. But to me, one of the most beautiful teachings about the revelation is that only the first letter of the first word was heard, and heard around the world. The first

Hebrew letter of the word *Anochi* is *alef*, which has no sound. More accurately, it is the sound of silence, the Inaudible. *Alef* is the number one, not the integer that is followed by two, but the One of totality and all inclusiveness, the One of the Infinite.

If a computer printer had been plugged in at Mount Sinai, it would still be printing out the data, the understanding and interpretation of the experience. In fact, it is still printing out today through the fantastic, unbroken flow of oral tradition. But we tend to lose ourselves in the understanding and interpretation or in the argument whether it is God revelation or man-written. And in almost all cases, the initiating experience is long forgotten.

PURSUING THE PRESENCE OF GOD

Eating from the fruit of the Tree of Knowledge of Good and Evil left us conceiving time as linear: What is past is past. We perceive Shabbat as the seventh day of the week. It follows the sixth day, Friday, and precedes the following first day, Sunday. But from the perspective of the Tree of Life, Shabbat is an ever-present dimension of time, the "ground" to the "figure" of the six days, just as the surface of my desk is always there though it is constantly covered up by the clutter of the everyday. So, too, the Inaudible Infinite *Alef* of revelation is eternal and ever-present but remains unheard and unseen and unknown due to the clutter of our minds.

But just as heart disease can be reversed by ceasing to ingest food that is high in fat and cholesterol, so too can we reverse spiritual heart disease by eliminating or at least by cutting down on the junk content of the things our eyes, ears, and minds take in, in our normal everyday diet of perceptions.

Judaism pursues the experience of the presence and revelation of God. Its primary practices of prayer, Shabbat, and learning are aimed at that. But without some ongoing connection to the nonlinear, the multidimensional, the Tree of Life, we forget about this other dimension of life. The real definition of being a slave, of being in exile, is learning about it but forgetting to experience it. Meditation is so important because it is a way back to the experience. It is the beginning of taking time to create the space to hear the Infinite Inaudible *Alef*. Jewish meditation not only lifts up the individual to the One, it brings us all back to being One with one another. It is the beginning of creating a new (though ancient) reference point to what is really the essence of our lives, to the point of living, to the ground of being. We can learn about it all we want, through philosophy, religion, or psychology, but until we reexperience it, we remain slaves to our enlightened ideas.

The commandment to keep Shabbat is a commandment to take time out, to meditate. It is nonnegotiable because it knows how clever the ego/mind is in creating excuses not to get to the core of your being.

MOVING TOWARD THE CENTER

Meditation does not mean sitting like a pretzel with your eyes closed. You can meditate sitting in a chair, standing, walking, dancing, or laying down. There are meditative practices to empty your mind completely or to focus your mind on one thing. It can be visual, aural—or whatever. It can be done through physical movement, emotions, thinking, learning, and contemplating. It can be done through art, music, or song.

The fact is that everyone needs some kind of access to this

deeper dimension and quality in their life. The vast variety of practices exists so that everyone can find their own way or ways. The most crucial factor that prevents most people from touching this dimension is time and their perceived lack of it.

The English word *meditation* comes from the Latin, *medi,* which means "center." It is why many people talk about getting "centered" when discussing meditation. It's a way to touch your center. But this concept still puts you at the center. Going a little higher, we find that it is also getting in touch with the center of all life, the purpose of being, the Consciousness in whose dream you are. In Hebrew, *Hitbonenut* means "contemplation," "to be alone," or "all-one" with God or what the late Shlomo Carlebach called "holy alone-ness." Many meditations teach a quieting of mind, watchfulness, mindfulness. The question is whether there is just the individual's own mindfulness to be achieved or whether the individual's mindfulness is permeated with God's "mindfulness."

USING THE FOUR WORLDS CONCEPT

The Jewish meditations with which I mainly work are based on ideas and maps of the Four Worlds, a kabbalistic concept. The Four Worlds are the World of Action; the World of Formation; the World of Creation; and the World of Emanation. The goal of these meditations is to facilitate the permutation of the more expanded levels of soul into your very physical sense of being and into your everyday activities. We strive to do this during worship with preliminary prayers that focus on the World of Action and the physical body and begin the process of opening to dimensions that we don't normally let through. Then, with *P'sukei D'zimrah,* the Psalms, we focus on the World of Formation, the "emotional body," letting it come through the physical and opening it up to the levels beyond it. Next, with the *Sh'ma*, we focus on the World of Creation, or the "mental body," helping it to come through the emotional and physical and opening it up to the influence and influx from beyond it. Finally, with the *Amidah*, we focus on the World of Emanation, the "spiritual body." Like the High Priest entering the Holy of Holies, we try to strip away our outer garments and put on the simple pure garment of the soul to be as selfless and humble as possible and to be more the godly life force that we truly are.

BRINGING GODLINESS INTO EVERYDAY LIFE

We build our spiritual "muscles" during prayer to become more and more transparent and present in all of our day-to-day transactions and interpersonal interactions. The goal of the Jewish meditation practices that I do is to bring godliness more into our everyday life and to see godliness in everyone around us. It is meditation in service of psychological unfolding. In turn, this psychological work advances our meditation.

Jewish meditation is a full-time process of working on our *midot*, our personality, so that each trait can be a channel for the highest aspect of that trait—its godly aspect—to come through. This is also the framework for the practices of the *mitzvot*, for *mitzvot* without godly character are not up to measure.

Jewish meditation aims not just to improve the individual or advance his or her release from this world of duality. It aims to fix and elevate this world, to sacralize the everyday. Our goal isn't to get "out of here," but to walk in a sacred manner, to bring godliness everywhere, and to perceive godliness everywhere. Psalm 16 says, "I hold God before me always." Hasidic practice understands this to mean, "I see God equally in everyone, everywhere, always." Quite a way to strive to live.

✳

Sylvia Boorstein is recognized as a teacher of Buddhism and mindfulness meditation, and is also an observant Jew. She is a cofounding teacher of Spirit Rock Meditation Center in Woodacre, California, and a senior teacher at the Insight Meditation Society in Barre, Massachusetts. She's the author of *It's Easier Than You Think: The Buddhist Way to Happiness; Don't Just Do Something, Sit There: A Mindfulness Retreat Manual;* and *That's Funny, You Don't Look Buddhist: On Being a Faithful Jew and a Passionate Buddhist* (HarperSanFrancisco). Boorstein's insights are useful to all meditation practitioners, regardless of their religious affiliation. She is concerned with bringing mindfulness to everyday experience.

---

11 On Mindfulness

SYLVIA BOORSTEIN

Early on in my mindfulness meditation practice, I spent several weeks in intensive retreat in a monastery in Massachusetts. In the weeks just before that retreat, the entire country had followed the story of a young child with leukemia whose parents, dedicated to alternative healing, had refused to accept conventional treatment for him. The child died. Since childhood leukemia has a high cure rate with modern medicines, I was very upset about what I considered the parents' "attachment to New Age views." I was more than upset; I was mad. "How could they do this?" I thought. I was infuriated, by extension, at everything that I associated with "New Age." I was mad at news-letters and magazines and books and diet regimens and health food stores—I was mad at anything I felt had colluded in form-ing these parents' attachment to a view I thought had cost the child his life. I also felt righteous in my anger, since I was, at that time, a vegetarian, a yoga teacher, and a meditation prac-titioner, and I thought I had made my choices wisely, while other people's narrow-mindedness and rigidity were giving my choices a bad name.

I arrived at the retreat troubled by my anger. It continued for days in spite of my attempts to develop composure. I'm fairly sure that the level of my anger was probably also sustained by my fear about what I considered inadequate parenting. At that time, I had young children of my own, and the idea that par-ents might be so trapped by views that they could make decisions that had such dire consequences frightened me. Every time I remembered the story, my mind filled with anger and indigna-tion and, finally, resentment that these parents, strangers to me, had "destroyed my retreat by their behavior." I felt so burdened that I prayed, "May I be *free* from this painful anger," asking that no reminder of the incident would arise in my mind to trigger another attack of anger.

One afternoon, sitting quietly, in a moment in which my mind was completely resting, an entirely new thought arose: "Those parents must be in terrible pain!" And then: "How are they going to live with themselves?" I was startled to find that my anger had disappeared. I still believed the refusal of medi-cine was a wrong choice, but I felt sad instead of mad and, at last, compassionate. "What if I made a terrible mistake—even a well-intentioned terrible mistake—with my children? I couldn't bear it."

At the moment of my change of heart, I was so grateful that I didn't think about how or why it had happened. I was just glad to have been set free. It felt like a miracle. I later discovered it is really not a miracle. It's the grace of mindfulness. Mindfulness meditation does not change life. It changes the heart's capacity to accept it. It teaches the heart to be more accommodating, not by beating it into submission, but by developing wisdom.

CULTIVATING A BALANCED AWARENESS

Mindfulness is a natural capacity of mind. It's balanced awareness of the truth of present experience. Our habitual responses to challenge are often flurried and create confusion. Mindfulness *practice* calms and steadies the mind so that confusion is recognized and clarity maintained.

I think of mindfulness as a practice that develops over time, as well as sufficient unto itself in every moment. It's *becoming* wise and *being* wise at the same time. The becoming wise aspect happens gradually. By paying attention calmly, in all situations, we begin to see clearly the truth of life experience. We realize that pain and joy are both inevitable and that they are also both time limited. We discover, more and more often, that struggling with what is beyond our control is extra. It creates suffering. We also discover that kind, considered responses make life manageable and leave room for compassionate response. The being wise part of mindfulness is balanced, alert, nonembittered responsiveness. Each moment of nonstruggle is a moment of freedom, a moment in which the mind, at ease, is able to access the truth of the moment clearly.

Although mindfulness is a natural capacity of the mind,

the pressures of daily life often present challenges to seeing clearly. A retreat provides a special opportunity to practice. When I began my practice twenty years ago, I had a family and a professional life that would not support extended periods of intensive meditation, so I incorporated shorter retreat periods into my life. Retreats are simple, nonsectarian, and open to students who are at all levels of experience, since the instructions remain the same throughout practice. Retreatants in a traditional mindfulness retreat spend their days alternating periods of sitting and walking meditation. Students are encouraged to bring calm attention to each moment of experience without adding to it. Often, they are given preliminary instructions that encourage focusing attention on the breath during sitting meditation or on physical sensations while walking. This particular attention to the essentially neutral activities of breathing and walking develops composure in the mind, which then supports the ability to pay balanced attention to the entire range of body and mind experience. When I finally understood that, years after I began meditating, my life became my practice.

MINDFULNESS AS WISDOM PRACTICE

My experience is that mindful awareness provides the context for religious expression. As I have been increasingly able to stay alert and balanced from moment to moment, the truths of impermanence, suffering, and the interconnectedness of all things have been revealed as "insights." As my insight developed, my suffering lessened. As it did, I became kinder, my prayers became more meaningful, and I have been sustained in my capacity to bless.

Mindfulness cultivates compassion. As I practiced, I saw

how the painful habit of clinging mind is very strong. I watched the way my mind made up extra stories, complicating my life and upsetting me unnecessarily. I also saw that even *awareness* of attachment causing suffering did not necessarily end it. I recognized that must be true for everyone and understood that the pain of the world is *enormous*. For some period of time, I was depressed with what seemed to me the inescapable sadness of life, and I felt heartbroken. The result of the heartbreak is that I became more compassionate to myself and to the other people in my life.

I first met Rabbi Mordechai Sheinberger in Jerusalem five years ago. I told him I was a meditation teacher. He asked about my practice and about what I taught. I explained mindfulness. He said, "Well, I'm not a meditation teacher. I teach the path of *mitzvot.*" On his suggestion, I read *The Path of the Just*, by Moses Chaim Luzzatto, an eighteenth-century Kabbalist, and found it an elaborate and inspiring framework of guides for behavior, all rooted in kindness. It seemed obvious to me that dedication to *mitzvot* practice requires *incredible* impeccability and scrupulous attention to the intention motivating every act, the basics of mindfulness meditation.

MINDFULNESS, PRAYER, AND MOMENTS OF BLESSING

I trust that prayer is the natural, legitimate, effective response to realizing the incomprehensibility of cosmic design. My prayer life became more real to me as I recognized that the things that made me happy were fundamentally a gift and beyond my control. All my previous hesitations, all my "logical" questions about prayer ("To whom?" "Does it work?") fell away. Prayers—

prayers of gratitude and even of supplication—became the voiced (silent or aloud) expression of the truth of my heart.

Judaism is a blessing religion, and mindfulness supports the capacity to bless at all times. Pleasant, fortunate situations inspire automatic blessing as thanksgiving. Painful situations are more challenging. The visceral response to acknowledging pain is recoil, aversion. The *mindful* response is compassion based in the wisdom that in a precise, just cosmos, *everything* is revelation of lawful order. A blessing practice holds the mind steady. A steady mind supports mindfulness. Mindfulness maintains clarity. Clarity reveals the truth of the cause-and-effect structure of creation's interconnectedness, awesome enough to inspire spontaneous blessing. Wisdom is the realm, I believe, in which blessings are kept alive.

✴

Steve Fisdel was ordained a rabbi by Zalman Schachter-Shalomi through P'nei Or (Renewal) in Philadelphia. He is the spiritual leader of Congregation B'nai Torah in Antioch, California. He serves several independent congregations in the San Francisco area, besides having a busy writing schedule. He is especially concerned with our ability to connect, through meditation, with the Divine, how this can be done, and the principles involved in doing so.

12 Meditation as Our Own Jacob's Ladder

RABBI STEVE FISDEL

The true, primary objective of meditative practice within Jewish tradition is *yichud*, unification with God. It is very important to remember that the soul is a reflection of a divine consciousness within the universe. We are told, specifically in Genesis, that we are made in the image of God. Our souls, therefore, are part of the divine level of created consciousness.

As sentient beings, we are acutely aware of our own uniqueness as individual souls. At the same time, we are aware of our separation from God, which is the basis for that uniqueness. As we struggle in our lives to express ourselves, our awareness of ourselves as individuals leading singular lives often makes us feel alone, disconnected, and uncertain. We experience isolation and fear and long to be reunited with the source of our being.

In Jewish mysticism, meditation can bridge this gap. In reality, nothing exists outside of God, and everything emanates directly from the Holy One. Human souls have a choice: we can focus on our own individuality and on our own will—or on being unique expressions of Divine will.

If we focus only on ourselves and our narrow, ordinary cognitive experience, we cripple ourselves spiritually. On the other hand, if we reconnect with God by a directed focus through meditation, we unite ourselves with the Source of all being and come to understand the greater dimensions of our lives.

We can focus on our physical lives and experience life linearly on the plane of cause and effect. Many people do this because they do not perceive another alternative. Or we can experience life as a fabric, in which our routine cognitive existence is a strand in a much broader mosaic of perception, understanding, and knowing. Through meditation, we can experience higher levels of reality and deeper layers of self. We can draw closer to God, and we can come to know who we truly are. We can connect with the Creator and know the Divine essence within ourselves.

The purpose of life is the evolution of consciousness. This is as true at the individual level of the soul as it is on the universal, cosmic plane. It means that our lives are a constant process of self-realization, emotional and psychological growth, and spiritual development. Through experience of life, we mature as souls.

Our developmental process can take the high road—or the low road. On the low road, we focus on the concrete, mundane level of physical existence and survival. On the high road, life is experienced on multiple levels of reality, and it is expanded by purposeful effort through meditation and continually strives to unite with God. That is why *yichud*, unifying with God, is the principal goal of Jewish meditation practice.

CULTIVATING PROPER PREPARATION

It is very important that those who meditate be properly prepared for it and know that they are opening inner doors that will alter their consciousness. These states are far deeper than any to which we are accustomed on the purely cognitive or emotional levels of daily life. We must be open to experiencing and accepting these experiences.

These points of consciousness are often discussed in Jewish mystic literature. Kabbalist literature has lengthy discussions on such subjects as the very process of Creation, the nature and dynamics of the soul, the unfolding of God's will within the cosmos and within human consciousness, the process of ascending to the Throne of God, reincarnation, dream realities, and the nature of good and evil.

Much of Kabbalist thought and doctrine attempts to systematically articulate knowledge gained from meditative experience. Over the centuries, a refined terminology and conceptual framework developed to help express what was experienced at levels of consciousness that had been reached through meditation.

Anyone can be trained to meditate. Its benefits are profound and deeply important at any stage of development and practice. Anyone who is interested should be encouraged to embark on this route of self-discovery and evolution. The caveat is that we must be ready to make a deep, personal commitment to meditate.

This discipline requires long-term commitment, consistent effort, devotion to God, and steadfast determination to work diligently on your own spiritual development. Meditative practice and self-understanding are mastered only by degrees. We cannot be impatient, seeking a quick fix to life through meditation, just as we cannot expect any real long-term benefit if we are inconsistent with our meditative practice. Meditation also requires studying traditional Kabbalist texts, which reflect the experience of earlier generations of meditators.

Once we understand these principles and undertake to learn and practice meditation, it does not matter at what point we begin. Our knowledge of Kabbalah, of meditation, and of Judaism will develop and expand naturally, just as we as meditators will develop and expand over time through our own experience. The level of our knowledge should never deter us from pursuing meditation as long as we understand what to expect and are willing to make the commitment and necessary effort and accompany that with the proper spiritual focus.

MAJOR SCHOOLS OF MEDITATION

There are a number of schools of thought in Kabbalah. Each school has generated a specific type of meditation practice suited to its own emphasis, experience, and viewpoint. Among the earliest schools were the *Maaseh Bereshith*, the Act of Creation, and the *Maaseh HaMerkavah*, the Action of the Chariot.

Maaseh Bereshith focuses on the process by which the universe and everything in it is created and sustained by God. It carefully details the process of Creation's unfolding and describes the progressive emanation of the universe from the moment of Divine thought to the actual materialization of the physical universe. This approach is expounded at great length in the Zohar, one of Kabbalah's greatest and most central works. The meditations that are linked to this school of thought center on the *sefirot*, the ten emanations or states of the creative process, that represent the flow of the Divine will from thought to materialization. The ten *sefirot* are linked together structurally in a paradigm known as the Tree of Life. Meditation from this perspective often involves focusing on the *sefirot* and their relationship to each other. The objective of this type of meditation is to gain greater insight and understanding into the creative process and the very structure of Creation.

Maaseh HaMerkavah, or Chariot mysticism, centers on ascending the higher levels of reality until we reach the highest level: the Throne of God, where the Presence of God, the Creator of the universe, is felt and experienced. The surviving literature of this early school of Kabbalist thought speaks often of what the soul will encounter at each level of the seven-stage journey from normal consciousness to the consciousness of the Throne level. In this type of meditation, the imagery of the texts and the names of the various angels associated with each level are used as the focal points of meditation.

The Kabbalists also taught that each of the twenty-two letters of the Hebrew alphabet represents a primal cosmic force that is a fundamental building block of Creation. Each letter is a different light, a different energy. The combination of any group of letters is understood to be an interaction of primal energies, the result of which is the emergence of some specific reality within the universe.

Whereas the *sefirot* are the stages of Creation, Hebrew letters are the structural elements linking the *sefirot* together into an intelligible system. Meditating on the Hebrew alphabet taps into the primal, creative forces that underlie the entire universe. Such meditative practices focus on deepening your understanding of the structure of Creation and the hidden relationships between all created things.

Of later origins is meditating on the *ayin*, on nothingness. This centers on the relationship between nonexistence and being. Jewish belief emphasizes that God continually creates the universe from nothingness. God continually is bringing existence forth from nonexistence.

The doctrines and meditations developed in the early eighteenth century by Rabbi Dov Baer of Mezritch and Rabbi Levi Yitzhak of Berditchev emphasize the importance of connecting with the undulation of nothingness and consciousness. Human consciousness oscillates between a state of void and a state of cognitive consciousness, the latter being born out of the former and then returning back to it. Among the later Hasidic masters, this approach produced meditative practices involving *Bittul*, the temporary negation of ego.

HOW TO ESTABLISH A MEDITATION PRACTICE

To establish a meditation practice, one must first become familiar with the various types of meditation that exist within Judaism. Some will seem more appealing than others. It is very important to find one specific type of meditation that truly resonates with you. Over time, you may find more than one type of meditation that you wish to include in your practice. It is, however, best to start with one, learn it, and experience it fully before moving on to another. You may have to try several types of meditation to determine that which is the most appropriate for you. Not everyone is suited to every type of meditation practice.

It is important to bear in mind that the various kabbalistic schools were established at different periods of time by mystics with diverse views and temperaments. The doctrines and practices of each school were meant for distinct audiences and designed to address different needs and interests.

If possible, you should work with someone who is experienced in Jewish meditation practice and who, at least initially, can guide you effectively. This may be done in a class setting, in an informal group structure, or through private instruction. If you are familiar with meditation from a different tradition, such as yoga or Sufism, it is easy to transfer those skills directly to Jewish meditation. Yet, even in this instance, having an experienced teacher introduce you to Jewish meditative practices is important in the early stages.

THE BEGINNING STAGES

In the beginning stages of practice, read material on basic Kabbalist thought and study the doctrines and techniques of Jewish meditation before attempting to practice it. Once you become more proficient, it is worthwhile to study more advanced books. Ultimately, as an advanced meditator, you may find that the texts themselves are the best guides for further development.

Another element of establishing a successful meditation practice is consistency. Meditation is a very private matter. The two terms in Hebrew for meditation both point in the same direction: *Hitbonenut,* which means "coming to know yourself," and *Hitbodedut,* which means "being alone." Being able to periodically meditate with others is an added benefit but not a substitute for personal work and discipline.

Meditation should be done when there is little possibility of external distraction. You need peace, calm, and total quiet to relax and concentrate. This is one reason that the Kabbalists said that midnight is the best time to meditate. You need not fix the hour of meditation specifically at midnight, but it should be when you can seclude yourself comfortably and not be bothered by outside thoughts, activities, or demands.

Meditation also requires a comfortable space and a physical environment conducive to relaxation, peace, and serenity. This can be a specific room or a partitioned area, one that is either a place permanently reserved for meditation or one that needs to be recreated as needed. It helps greatly to go to a place that is familiar, safe, and peaceful when exploring other states of consciousness.

Controlling one's environment during meditation also means being able to prevent any possible interruptions from taking place. If necessary, lock the door, turn off the telephone and the computer, and lower the lights. Candles can create focal points of light and give off soft energy. Incense and flowers stimulate olfactory centers and trigger emotion. Music, chanting, or tonal patterns can influence moods and alter perceptions. Create the proper environment, and work regularly with the practices you have selected.

THE FOUR GATES OF MEDITATION— THE STAGES OF DEVELOPING A MEDITATION PRACTICE

When initiating a meditation practice, know the phases you may experience and the obstacles you might face. As you begin meditation, you will pass through four gates. First is the Gate of

Confusion, which occurs as you begin experiencing meditative states and you start moving beyond the conventional pattern of life. It is easy at this point to become disoriented, confused, and even frightened. What you experience will be new and unfamiliar. It may even run contrary to beliefs you have held dear all your life. You may begin to doubt yourself: Am I losing my mind? How can I tell what is real and what is imagined? Is this a connection to a new level of understanding or only to subconscious material?

To move past this first stage, trust yourself and the integrity of what you are experiencing. Learn to disconnect the ego from the meditation process, thereby putting the fears and doubts behind you. This requires learning to distinguish what you are experiencing from how you interpret the experience.

Once you master your fear and doubt, you will pass through the Gate of Emotion, which requires handling powerful feelings. Experiencing levels of consciousness that are so much vaster than our normal, waking consciousness opens emotional channels—fear, joy, exhilaration. It takes time to learn how to control this flood of emotion. This is particularly true if you repressed emotions in the past because these will flood to the surface once the gates are opened.

Once you become familiar with controlling the emotions, you reach the Gate of Transformation, perhaps the hardest and certainly the most important gate. Here, your belief system collapses. What you believed about the nature of reality, about yourself, about life, and about purpose now must be discarded in the face of new experience emanating from higher dimensions of consciousness.

Beginning meditators must learn to release the old, rigid structures of belief and embrace their new experiences, allowing them to continually modify their awareness and understanding. Learning to always be open to continual change is the last gateway: the Gate of Being. At this point, you cease to be a meditator seeking enlightenment and become a consciously evolving soul. Rather than being a "path," meditation becomes a part of life, as natural and vital a process as breathing and the continual basis of your spiritual evolution.

In Judaism, meditation is neither a simple activity nor a means to an end. It is Jacob's ladder, connecting heaven and earth for those who are prepared to continually ascend and descend through higher states of consciousness. Jewish meditation, like any other aspect of Judaism, is a way of life. It is a way of expressing who you are, of continually affirming your commitment to God. If you understand this deep in the recesses of your heart, then Jewish meditation can provide a solid cornerstone for your spiritual growth.

✳

Shefa Gold received her ordination from The Reconstructionist Rabbinical College and currently lives in a retreat center on top of a mountain in New Mexico. She was one of the very first people in the United States to begin the arduous task of reinvigorating the art of Jewish chant—not chant in the more mechanical way of the normal synagogue service, but as a holy, ecstatic experience. This teaching seeks to define the power and place chant holds within the Jewish meditation teaching tradition.

---

13 That This Song May Be a Witness: The Power of Chant

RABBI SHEFA GOLD

Like many Jews, I am a lover of words. I loved Hebrew, even when I didn't "understand" a word of it. The sounds seemed to open up the place inside me that wanted to pour itself out to God. They turned me inside out in ways that made me feel visible to God so I could be seen and known and loved. As my love for the sounds grew along with my knowledge of Hebrew words, I found myself seriously out of step with formal communal prayer. My thirst to drink deeply from certain phrases in the liturgy that called to me was constantly being frustrated by the pace and volume of traditional prayer. I began to look for what was essential in prayer and to search for the deep structure of the prayer service that would help me understand the function, and not merely the content, of each prayer. My background in music and many forms of meditation prepared me in developing a changing practice that treated the sacred phrase as a doorway. Repetition became a way to still the mind and open the heart so widely that it felt as if the sacred phrases were planting seeds there.

THE CHANT AND ITS POWER

The power of the chant can help connect members of a group to each other. This is especially important during a prayer service, since it allows us to pray in the voice of community as well as from an individual perspective. It is important to gradually connect one's solitary meditative practice with formalized communal prayer so that the spiritual benefit from one can inform the other.

In Deuteronomy 31, God instructs Moses to "write this song for yourselves and teach it to the Israelites; put it in their mouths, that this song may be a witness...." But God predicts that when the people enter the Land, they will "get fat"; that is, they will become complacent and forgetful and break the covenant. Yet, though they might ignore every teaching of God, the song that has been planted within them will not be forgotten. It will serve as a reminder and a witness to help redirect their hearts toward the One God.

Chanting cultivated in me a garden of devotion, yearning, joy, and vision—reminders of my connection to God. Gradually, I became familiar with the wide range of mind states that the chants engendered. At first, I was drawn especially to ecstatic states, which were both healing and empowering. But at some point, I became less attached to those states and began to notice the silence that followed the chant. I felt drawn into that silence. I had known that the chant was a doorway, but before I really understood the invitation of the silence, I had not really crossed the threshold.

ENTERING THE *MISHKAN*

Being drawn into the space within, learning to enter it without disturbing its form, is similar to entering the *mishkan*, the Tabernacle in the desert. The Book of Exodus describes the tender care and great attention to detail that was exhibited while building the *mishkan*—the artistry, skill, inventiveness, and sheer generosity. When I lead chanting, I feel like Bezalel, the chief artist of the *mishkan*. I direct a "building project" whose purpose is to create a dwelling place for God in our community, in our hearts.

Learning each particular state of mind that is possible to attain through a certain chant is part of this project. As I expand my repertoire of meditative tools, I also deepen my connection to tradition and especially to the prayer service so I can trust the power of prayer and integrate the teachings of Torah into my heart, which has been opened by that power.

Another piece of this work is understanding and using the interdependent relationship between the "ecstatic" and the "contemplative." The ecstatic component of chant lets me move into a contemplative space that has been strengthened by the fullness of my devotion. Chanting within the context of contemplative silent practice creates a space in which the power of the chant deepens and evolves, allowing its potential to unfold in the silence. My intention is not for the chant to continue in the silence, but rather for the chanter to use the chant as a doorway into the depths and the vast expanse of the silence.

YIELDING TO THE POTENTIAL
OF EACH MOMENT

In developing a chant, I first choose a phrase from a text that speaks to me with beauty or mystery. I pay close attention not just to the meaning of the words, but also to the sounds and the feelings they evoke. I've learned that certain sounds powerfully affect the mind, heart, or body and that certain rhythms of breathing can produce specific states of mind. I've learned to expand the range of "tones" that will inspire and evoke memory, meaning, and depth. I've learned that the power of the chant can sometimes be increased by certain visualizations or body movements. I work with the tools that I know so well—melody, harmony, syncopation—yet I don't use them just to make something that is pleasing or beautiful. A chant is not a song.

The difference between chanting and singing is crucial. Chanting is primarily a meditative process. It requires an inward focus, a sensitivity to the energy of the group and a willingness to serve the group. Through chanting, all these foci are cultivated and strengthened. As with any type of meditation, effort is required. Yet at some point, you must simply surrender to the power of the chant, to the Divine Presence, and to the transformation in you.

Here is an example of a chant and how it might be used. It consists of a phrase from Psalm 23: *Kosi R'vaya,* which is often translated as "My cup runneth over." In introducing the chant to a class, I try to bring its context to life: Though I walk through the valley of the deepest darkness, I will not fear evil, for You, God, are with me. How do You manifest yourself to me? I have come face-to-face with my own demons across the lavish table that You spread before me. And on that table is a cup that is overflowing.

In building the *kavvanah*, the intention, for this chant, I invite participants to appreciate two different dimensions of "cup." One cup is located in the heart. It is the connection to the source of Life and Love within us, and no matter what befalls us or what "enemy" faces us from across "the table," that inner cup continues to flow—and then to overflow. The sound of the chant reconnects us to that flow.

The other "cup" is the cup that is formed in community. The sound of our voices and the strength of our shared intention create that cup, which contains the Divine flow that nourishes us. As we form the cup of community, we enable each person to access exactly what they need and to drink from the flow that we create together.

This chant is composed of three parts. Different rhythmic patterns evoke the feeling of rivulets flowing mellifluously together, then apart. Chanting is done with eyes closed to promote greater concentration and less self-consciousness. The chant moves through several phases as the community gradually surrenders to its flow and as each heart begins to open in response to its gentle beauty. If people feel emotions welling up in them as they chant, they are instructed to pour that energy into the chant, in service to the group, and to let go of each thought or feeling as it arises. Each repetition is an opportunity to be more present, to bring more attention to listening and receiving the "whole" of the chant, and to refining one's own intention and generosity.

It is the leader's responsibility to understand the direction, the function, and the potential of the chant in the context of a worship service or a group meditation and to know when to end it. Often, some chant leaders will end a chant too soon or when normal consciousness is threatened. The goal is to chant through our boredom or through the anxiety of losing control or losing the fixed boundaries of self. At that point, there is a sudden expansion in consciousness and a cohesion of the group. The most powerful moment of the chant happens in the silence that follows its conclusion. Then, the chant inclines the mind toward a certain state of consciousness. Chanting teaches how to discern the potential of that moment and how we can let its fullness unfold as we walk through the door it opens. Key to using that energy is a willingness to serve and to surrender one's "personal" experience. Thus, the self expands beyond its normal boundaries, and there is a taste of connection. In order to grow beyond just tasting, one must encounter certain obstacles to practice and be careful of certain traps that lie along the way.

SIDESTEPPING OBSTACLES ON OUR WAY TO PRAYER

I distinguish between obstacles and traps. It's important to identify both. Sometimes I look at my spiritual practice as a search for the right balance between "surrender" and "will." The will is expressed through our commitment to rigor, regularity, moving through difficult places, expending effort, not giving up. Each of us faces such obstacles as laziness, apathy, confusion, loneliness, despair, or cynicism. Our will can make us feel that we are in perfect control and that spiritual attainments are within our grasp. When we get so caught up in the power of the will, our egos take over and eventually exclude the flow of Divine Grace that can unite us with each other.

The main obstacle to surrender is fear: Fear of the unknown. Fear of letting go. Fear of not being "in control." Fear of opening up to an insight that will compel us to change. The trap of surrender comes in not being able to discern inner voices, of following blindly, and of rejecting the responsibility of becoming a partner with God rather than merely remaining God's subject.

All spiritual practice brings us face-to-face with our particular resistance. By doing so, we come to know ourselves; with that knowledge comes the growth of compassion and spiritual power. It's important to remember that resistance isn't what keeps us from our spiritual work. It is the work. Sometimes what we most yearn for is also what we are most afraid of. Chanting is powerfully effective in awakening that yearning and in giving us the energy and courage to face our fears. The danger in spiritual practice is that each of us has our "blind spots" regarding either the nature of resistance or our particular trap. Having a spiritual friend or a teacher to help us through those blind spots is important. Just knowing that those blind spots exist can help keep us humble and careful.

My own chanting evolved from searching for a form of prayer that would let me experience the Divine and would deepen and develop with practice. Indeed, the experience of chant has enhanced my silent meditative practice. My "base" practice remains the same and is the foundation for other practices that evolve and change according to whatever I feel is needed. That core practice is a silent, twenty-minute daily meditation that I call *devekut* (cleaving). It is a practice of intention. My intention is to be in God's presence and to gently let go of all thoughts that may arise that take me from God's presence. One of the purposes of this meditation is to develop an ongoing, vital relationship with the Divine, which then becomes the foundation for prayer. I believe that different forms of Jewish meditation can strengthen one's prayer life. When I work with a sacred phrase from the liturgy, exploring its meaning with the intuitive senses of the heart and letting that meaning expand and affect my inner life, then that phrase has a new power for me. The cumulative experience of using many phrases from the siddur (the prayer book) in meditation gradually injects new life and new depth into prayer.

In leading a chanting service, I study the week's Torah portion for its spiritual challenge. With that in mind, I build the *kavvanah* (passionate intentionality) for the change I seek in ways that will inspire a "rising to meet" that challenge. A chanting service can help the traditional prayer service become a vehicle for healing, self-expression, visioning, inner journeying, and connection to ourselves, to each other, to the community, to the world, and to God.

✳

Sheila Peltz Weinberg was ordained by The Reconstructionist Rabbinical College and heads the Jewish Community of Amherst congregation in Amherst, Massachusetts. She is well-known for her work in leading discussions between Buddhists and Jews about meditation. Here, Rabbi Weinberg addresses the need to bring meditation more into mainstream Jewish practice and to welcome influences from other traditions, as long as they don't conflict with basic Jewish doctrine.

---

14 Meditating as a Practicing Jew

RABBI SHEILA PELTZ WEINBERG

In 1986, after my graduation from rabbinical school, I planned to visit a close friend in western Colorado who is a meditator. Our intention was to go together to a ten-day meditation retreat. I had been thinking about this since I had met her several years before in Jerusalem. The thought of being in silence was profoundly attractive to me, especially after four years in rabbinical school. Overstuffed with words, ideas, arguments, liturgies, and texts, I felt that information had crowded my mind and heart. I craved emptiness and space.

On the way to her home, I visited a friend. In a short time, friendship turned into romance, and he suggested that I spend the ten days with him in the mountains, hanging out and having fun. Why should I subject myself to the austere discipline and rigidity of a meditation retreat? "Not talk for ten days? That's crazy." There was enough skepticism and doubt in my mind and enough fantasy about the possibilities between myself and this man that I convinced myself to bypass the retreat in favor of the fling.

It took another four years for me to get the silence.

When I interviewed to be the rabbi of the Jewish community of Amherst, Massachusetts, the head of the committee was a wonderful man who was a lay leader of Insight Meditation Society (IMS) in Barre, Massachusetts, a retreat center less than an hour from Amherst. IMS was founded in the 1970s by three Jews—Joseph Goldstein, Jack Kornfield and Sharon Salzberg—who had studied and practiced with various Buddhist masters in Asia. They were trying to bring and adapt Buddhist teachings to the West. I did not acknowledge it fully to myself at the time, but this connection between the Jewish community in Amherst and IMS influenced my decision to move from Philadelphia to Amherst. In the summer of 1990, I signed up for a ten-day meditation retreat at IMS. This time, nothing deterred me. It was an intense experience.

THE STEPPINGSTONES OF MY SPIRITUAL PATH

When people speak about being on a spiritual path, I often wonder how to date the beginning of that path. Sometimes, I believe it begins at birth and only ends at death. Or does it have to do with meeting a teacher? Or with realizing a truth or an insight? Or with committing to a particular practice? Or having an experience of some sort? The one thing of which I am quite certain is that a spiritual path only seems like a path, a coherent journey, when one pauses and looks back. Then the pivotal points of revelation become vividly connected to one another. My spiritual path might have begun at Camp Ramah when I learned to pray with deep *kavvanah* (attention to the meaning) from a prayer book and heard God speaking to me from the prophetic books. Or it could have been after the birth of my daughter when I took a karate class and experienced in the very fibers of my body the connection between concentration, focus, breath, and power. I realized mind and body were not distinct. Or it could have been a month after the 1973 Yom Kippur War in Jerusalem when I took LSD for the only time in my life. I felt a wholeness and unity, a peace and contentment, a belonging and love that was new and beautiful. Or it could have been after the birth of my son in Scranton, Pennsylvania, when I walked into a group studying the teachings of Gurdjieff. I heard that the many aspects of my personality were temporary and unreliable but that I possessed an essential nature that was whole and pure and connected to the essential energy of the universe. Or was it when I was given the faith and courage to let go of a destructive addiction through the wisdom of a twelve-step program and an amazing woman named Grace? Or when I met Reb Zalman and heard him sing and teach and pull the many worlds together? Or was it the first time I saw a woman wearing a *tallit* and I realized that Judaism could be totally mine? Or the first class I attended on feminism and Judaism, when I was filled with the beauty and strength of my sisters who were entering an ancient stream and filling in the empty spaces with our own songs and stories and lives?

I do know that all of these moments came with me to my first meditation retreat and were the steppingstones of my spiritual path. In the silence at the retreat, I watched my mind, my feelings, and the sensations in my body coming and going, coming and going. Rather than be absorbed and distracted with work, conversations, and just plain busyness, the structure of the day was simple. There was no media, no written materials, no idle conversation. The only speaking was done by the teachers. We were encouraged to adopt a benevolent attitude toward everything we saw, which simply *was*. We were encouraged not to hold onto the pleasant or push away the unpleasant and instructed not to evaluate or judge the quality of our experience, but merely to observe it, to return to the moment, to dwell in bare attention.

SEARCHING FOR MYSELF

There was an enormous amount to hear in the silence. At first, much of it seemed frightening and distressing. My mind wanted to judge my achievement and success. I wanted to know how I was doing in relation to the others. Neither my thoughts, feelings, nor bodily sensations were under my control. In fact, I could hardly say they belonged to me. And who was "me," anyway? Sometimes my mind would drift into fanciful tales, bizarre movies with unknown characters and macabre plots. My mind rated and judged everything—the food, the thoughts themselves, the feelings, the other people, and mostly my performance. I was distraught at not having the usual diversions, the usual places to hold onto, and my mind would get caught in desire and control and aversion and the need for approval.

More than a few times during that first retreat, I prayed for deliverance. Maybe a note would be posted on the bulletin board for me saying there was an emergency at home and I had to leave. So what kept me there? It was the teachers' talks and their guidance and my own awareness that I was being healed and awakened through this process. The dharma talks primarily cited the teachings of the Buddha, but, to me, they reflected the wisdom of Torah and the twelve steps. I translated these spiritual vocabularies back and forth. Meditation, silence, and simplicity all offered an opportunity to test all the spiritual insights I had ever learned and to see how fleeting life is. They let me see how suffering grows from wanting what we don't have, from struggling with reality, from doubt and fear and the seduction of being separate, different, better or worse than everyone else. I heard the serpent speaking in my own mind, "You can be God. You can have it your way."

If these voices were not my true self, then who was I? The prayer book says that "the whole earth is filled with Her presence." When I touch the present moment, when the ego is not trapped in schemes of separation and justification, when the energy that unifies all creation is palpable, there is a sense of connection, peace, and deep happiness. This is what is eternal. That is who I am.

My first meditation retreat was a rocky road. There were moments of terrible loneliness, of seeing how needy I could be. And there were moments of revelation, of feeling that I was walking with God and breathing the breath of all life. Since then I have gone on three more ten-day retreats and one month-long retreat. Each has been deeply rewarding despite the pain of witnessing my ego's resistance to life. And each allows a glimpse into the perfection of what is that so often eludes my perception.

BLENDING JUDAISM AND DHARMA

After talking with Joseph Goldstein about why so many of the foremost Buddhist meditation teachers in the United States were Jewish and why great numbers of Jews practice Buddhist meditation, a few of us organized a conference for Jews interested in meditation, especially Buddhist meditation. This led to a retreat held every fall at the Barre Center for Buddhist Studies, led by Sylvia Boorstein and myself. We gather on Thursday for a day of mindfulness meditation. This leads into a Shabbat celebration that includes traditional prayers and Torah study as well as periods of silence. The silence and the meditation support Shabbat itself, which is really about letting go into pure being. Meditation is also about letting go: letting go of preconceived ideas and gently bringing oneself into the presence of what is, not what we imagine or remember or desire. Shabbat, like meditation, offers us a structure within which we can feel safe enough to let go—let go of our striving, our efforts to change things, our fears that there won't be enough, our urge to control the outcome of what we do.

A significant part of each retreat is a discussion of how one can be a practicing, believing Jew and still maintain one's love of the dharma (the spiritual path as taught by the Buddha) and commitment to meditation. Are these paths in conflict? I don't think so. Most Jews who become involved in Buddhist meditation are really not looking for a new religion. There is no effort at the retreats I have attended to convince participants to become anything or to assume a new identity. If anything, the practice is about letting go of habitual identities and unexamined labels. Many Jews are amazed and pleased when they discover that meditation and the insights that arise from it are authentic to Judaism, and they may lead them to explore traditional Jewish meditation techniques and practices.

BLENDING JUDAISM AND MEDITATION PRACTICE

I am particularly interested in seeing how the words of Jewish prayer, texts, and themes of Shabbat, festivals, and life cycle events reveal and reinforce the wisdom obtained in a meditation practice.

One example is the morning blessings. These fundamental parts of our daily liturgy have a powerful resonance when understood in the light of a meditative practice. For instance: We praise God for making us in God's image. But by being quiet and observing ourselves, we learn much about the laws of nature and the way things are. We see the effects of desire and the transformations of love. We see how struggle and resistance lead to more struggle and resistance and how acceptance and awareness liberate us. We encounter our compassion which is rooted in the eternalness of *chesed* (loving-kindness), which unites us with all that lives and never passes away because "love is [indeed] stronger than death." We praise God in that same litany, "who has provided for all my needs." In quiet contemplation, we see how our wants are not met and cannot be met because they are always changing. We may seek the newest car, a word of approval, or the latest book or film. We see how the I, the manifestation of self, passes away with the object it desires and is soon replaced by a new desire and a new self. We recognize that we already have that which sustains life and all of our basic needs. For this, our hearts leap in appreciation. And as they do, we feel compassion. We are in a state of great mind, *mochin gadlut*, as the Jewish mystics would say.

In the same liturgy, we praise God who guides human beings. As we practice letting go in meditation, we recognize that our job in life is to do what we are capable of doing. We are not in charge of the direction our life follows. We see this every time we sit down to be quiet. We never know what will be present. This experience of not knowing gives us a deeper insight into this wonderful daily blessing. Meditation can also give us a deeper understanding of the meaning of freedom. Freedom is central to being a Jew. We usually associate freedom with historical freedom and social justice. But communal freedom is a complement of inward freedom, of spiritual freedom. On Passover and on Shabbat and in every reference in the liturgy to the Exodus from Egypt, we are called to freedom. The practice of seeing the conditioned mind, of closely observing how habitual and automatic are our thoughts, feelings, and actions, is a practice of liberation. Through it, we liberate ourselves from fear, constant craving, and endless, pitiless judgment. As we do this, we are better able to look upon each other with generosity and inflict less harm on ourselves and each other.

The work of *tikkun olam* (repairing the world) and social justice depends on individuals who have looked at their own internal demons and are growing beyond their greed and self-centeredness. The inner work of spiritual freedom naturally leads to a desire to heal and serve. What seems like a solitary and remote practice—sitting in silence—actually thrives on the support of like-minded comrades and friends, the sharing of understanding and the developing of intimate relationships based on empathy, listening, and trust.

At one retreat, I had the idea to bring other rabbis to a silent retreat. The life of the rabbi is so intense, so noisy, so filled with words, prayers, and teaching that it is easy to become saturated. It is easy to lose oneself in the role and the expectations and the projections of others. Time together in silence for prayer, walking, sitting meditations, gentle guidance, and support could be enormously nurturing and supportive. So far, Sylvia Boorstein and I have led two three-day silent meditation retreats for rabbis. Everybody jokes, "You mean rabbis are going to get together and stay quiet for three days? Never." But it works—and it's a gift to them and to their congregations.

In the silence, we touch truths that we cannot express in words, truths that were the experiences of the poets and sages who wrote our prayers and blessings. In the silence, we feel our gratitude rising. The "hallelujah" we say is carried on the wings of a new connection and appreciation for the gifts of a life we have the calm and attention to really notice.

CREATING A TORAH COMMENTARY
FOR POST-MODERNS

Interweaving meditation and Judaism is part of creating a new *perush*, or commentary on Torah, for our post-modern age. Part of the *perush* which draws heavily on mystical and Hasidic Judaism, embraces the non-Jew, the woman, gays, and lesbians. Part of it is devoted to developing new leaders who are, most of all, practitioners of Judaism as a spiritual path. These leaders can inspire, but they will not be vicarious Jews for others. They will point the way but not take responsibility for getting anyone anywhere. Everyone must accept total responsibility for their own Jewish life and their own spiritual life and for doing the necessary work along the way. In this new paradigm, there may be quite a bit of divergence in personal practice. *Mitzvot* will be seen as precepts, as necessary structures for a disciplined spirituality, and as mirrors for us to see our capacity to surrender as well as our resistance and fear. New forms will continue to develop, such as intensive Jewish meditation retreats. In this new paradigm, there will be no tension between the inner work of renewal, silence, purification, and inspiration and the outer work of social change, challenging injustice, and defending the weak, the powerless, and the marginal.

Judaism has often benefited from its surrounding culture. We can choose to integrate into our Jewish lives the best of the surrounding culture—or the worst. I believe that meditation and silence offer us the best. Living in a troubled, violent, and uncertain time, we need desperately to focus our energies on that which most generates connection, peace, truth, and harmony. We need to find the abiding home of the soul, the place where God dwells always. It is from that home that our personal and collective life will flourish and grow.

✳

Laibl Wolf teaches Kabbalah and psychology at retreats and seminars internationally. He is an Orthodox rabbi, a lawyer, a spiritual counselor and the founder of the Human Development Institute in Australia. His concern is the misunderstandings that have developed about Jewish meditation and how so few people realize how fully developed this tradition is within Judaism.

15 Meditation and the Art of Growing Your *Neshamah*

RABBI LAIBL WOLF

It struck me as odd that some of my fellow Jews should discover spirituality in the Himalayas; not that I doubted the excitement it provided for some and the serenity it provided for others. It was, however, incongruous to me that the oldest of all peoples should become so disconnected from its roots, so utterly oblivious to its immense spiritual heritage that it had to look to the East to find its soul.

I was not jealous that the gurus of the East had become teachers of my searching coreligionists. Nor was I possessive of my soul brothers and sisters. Rather, I felt a sense of failure that we had failed to transmit the peace and happiness so many obviously yearned for.

There are many excuses for this, not the least of which is the horrific breach of continuity that the Holocaust had wrought.

Our masters had perished in the thousands. For every guru in the East, there had been dozens of rebbes in the West. Nearly all had perished. Our spiritual head had been decapitated.

NOT SO STRANGE WISDOMS

So when I met some Israelis in my native Melbourne, Australia, one sunny *Shabbos* afternoon while walking back from *shul*, my life changed dramatically. After I heard them talking in Hebrew, I invited them home for a *Shabbos* meal. Perhaps it was the idea of a *Dati* ("religious one") inviting a *Chiloni* ("secular one") that gave them a moment of pause before their uncertain acceptance of my invitation.

It transpired that they were returning from India, which had become a well-trodden route young Israelis traveled after their military service in Israel. They shared with me the wisdom they had acquired in the Himalayas. It occurred to me that while they had wandered far from Sinai—these wisdoms were not strange. I pulled Jewish texts from my shelves and pointed to pages that had the same ideas we were discussing. At first, my guests were somewhat puzzled. Why were Eastern truths written in their native Hebrew? Terms like *karma, bardo, reincarnation* suddenly materialized as *Schar* and *Onesh, Nisyonot, Gilgul Hanefesh, Hashgachah Pratit*. One of my guests became angry. His words ring in my ears even now: "Why have I, raised in Israel, educated in the Jewish education system, never encountered any notion of Jewish spirituality?" I had no answer that was palatable to my troubled guest.

Right there, my life changed: I became a poor man's Reb Zusya, a wandering minstrel of Hasidic spirituality. I flew thousands of miles, then drove thousands more in Australia's outback and coastal plains looking for counterparts to my Israeli guests—and I found hundreds of them. Then, I became more adventurous and began traveling through America with the same goal. I discovered that Jews are very ready to discover their spiritual roots, that they are ready for the discipline of meditation and to lead lives of purposeful discipline and self-mastery.

The major obstacle is that our spiritual leaders are holding back through confusion and fear. Thank God, there are a few exceptions to the rule, and their singular efforts are creating veritable waves.

There is good reason why some Jews look eastward. The Torah tells us that Abraham sent away his son whom he begot through his wife Hagar to the land of the East. He gave parting gifts. The deeper commentaries inform us that the land of the East was *Hodu*—India—and that these gifts were insights into the higher spiritual realms.

When I tell Hasidic tales about the reincarnation of a Jewish soul as a sheaf of wheat or a drop of water, I often hear, "But isn't reincarnation a Hindu or a Buddhist teaching?!" That may well be so, but remember, when the wisdom of the East was beginning to be formulated, there had already been a highly developed Jewish civilization for thousands of years!

THE COMMON UNDERLYING TRUTH OF ONENESS FOR DIFFERENT "FAMILIES" OF SOULS

But it does not really matter who came first. The true issue is that there is an understanding common to the East and to Judaism that testifies to the common underlying truth of Oneness. But please note, I say Oneness, not "sameness." Indeed, the soul systems that God created are not the same. There are families of souls, each with their different "spiritual diets." Am I talking about Jewish superiority? Chosen-ness? The People of the Book? No, I am talking about the beauty of differentness! When I shared this teaching with the Dalai Lama recently, he smiled and spoke of a universal pathway. The universal pathway certainly exists, through the seven Noachide Laws that govern a just and moral society. But we cannot escape the obvious truth that God seems to have had a predilection for creating a world of differentness. No two people have ever lived who are the same. No two snowflakes have fallen that have identical geometric internal structures. Our spiritual teachings inform us that the finite physical world is merely an analog of spiritual realm. The founder of Hasidism taught that to discover the nature of the upper realms, we must take a good look into our very selves. Therefore, although each soul is a distinct spiritual entity unlike any other soul, there are nevertheless "families" of souls. It is essential to realize that much of the rediscovery of meditation comes from our own ancient teachings. It is also essential to realize that not all meditations of the East suit the Jewish "family" of souls and that not all the Jewish meditations suit the many non-Jewish families of souls.

THE HIDDEN WORLD OF EVERYDAY REALITY

Many Eastern meditations are the product of a realization that this world is an illusion—*samsara* or *maya*. Judaism also recognizes that this realm of our consciousness is false. We call it *Olam Hasheker*, the "false world"! Indeed, the Hebrew word for "world"—*olam*—has a truer translation in "hidden." We recognize that this is the hidden realm. But here much commonality with the East ends. Judaism emphasizes that our primary agenda is to operate at the seemingly mundane, corporeal realm, albeit in an enlightened state. The ordinary is another word for the mundane. The kabbalistic work *Sefer Yetzirah (Book of Creation)* is attributed to Abraham. In it you will find the following teaching: "The end is wedged in the beginning, and the beginning is wedged in the end." This teaching can be understood in this way: An architect wakes up one night with an inspiration for a design. The next day, he instructs the draftspersons to prepare the plans. The plans eventually are submitted to the town planning permit committee. Then comes the excavation activity and building works. Some nine months down the track, you and I, passing by the beautiful structure, through its beauty gain a sense of that inspirational moment in the mind of the architect nine months earlier.

WHY ENGAGE IN MEDITATION

The whole purpose of the creation of human beings is the end product of *an ordinary world*. We must not escape this higher purpose by spending unnecessary time navel gazing and "ego-exploring" the higher realms. So why engage in meditation at all? It could be said that it is contrary to the Divine intent, which is that we remain grounded in the ordinary world. The answer lies in the uniquely Jewish teaching of *mitzvot,* deriving from the Aramaic *tzavta,* or "connection." The 613 *mitzvot* are points of connection to the *Ein Sof,* the Infinite Godhead. Through the practice of a *mitzvah,* our *neshamah,* or "soul," is raised to a higher awareness of itself and realizes its intimacy with *Hashem* (God). A sustained practice of *mitzvot* will heighten our inner awareness. Such mindfulness will create true awareness of the infinite cause and effect our behavior produces. This description of *mitzvot* may seem almost Buddhist-like. Some might even think that I have deliberately couched the description in Eastern terms to attract your attention. If it were not for the literally hundreds of ancient Jewish texts that speak in the same terms, there might be justification for such suspicions.

The practice of *mitzvot* unites the inner self with the Cosmic Self. It increases proficiency in self-mastery so that the activity of *mitzvot* is associated with the appropriate *kavvanah*, or holy intention and focus, to create inner balance and cosmic balance.

Many Jewish books testify to Jewish meditation as the wings that facilitate flight through higher realms, out-of-body experiences, soul-like astral projection. But these books must be read in the context of the times that they were written. Even some of Rambam's pronouncements on medicine or science can be set aside as new scientific data render them obsolete. Similarly, the purpose of meditation varies as the light of a new dawn demands change of purpose.

THE PURPOSE OF JEWISH MEDITATION

Meditation can too easily become "fool's gold." Individuals may spend day after day in meditational practice, exploring their "higher selves," but still behave obnoxiously to others. Even spiritual endeavor can be ego-centered or what Hasidism calls full of "*yeshut*" (full of oneself). To soar on high without a healthy purpose guided by a *mashpiah,* a spiritual mentor, yields falsehood in the guise of enlightenment.

My master, the Lubavitcher Rebbe, taught me that the purpose of Jewish meditation is to change one's nature and become a balanced, integrated individual. While many Eastern paths teach how to empty the mind, much Jewish meditation is geared to the filling of the mind through what we call *Hitbonenut.* Each path is specifically designed to address the *neshamah*'s foray through the labyrinth of the body. Its expression through the "container" (read "physiology") of the brain results in the process of mind or intellect. Its pathway through the metaphoric heart results in emotion. Mind and emotion are the product of ten spiritual godly emanations that transcend the four parallel spiritual realms. We are a swirling vortex of combinations and permutations of these ten basic emanations—the 'stuff' of Creation. Through exercising our *ratzon*, our higher will, we keep reforming the spiritual swirl within us into new shapes and potential. We call this the formation of thought, speech and behavior, which constantly create a new reality, not just for us, but for the cosmos as a whole. As the Baal Shem Tov taught, "The leaf falling off the tree is an intended and deliberate *Hashgachah* [act of godly intent] without which the cosmos would have veered off onto a wildly variant future line."

Can you imagine how our thoughts, words, and actions keep reshaping our inner spiritual shape and the consequent shape of all the higher realms? Can we afford not to engage in self-mastery appropriate to our soul system? A Jew has to relearn how to think, how to speak, and how to behave. A behavioral approach, which is the system of Hasidic meditation that I teach, is the basis of the Jewish meditational foci.

Of course, a Jew involved in Buddhist practice can become more aware and gentle. And a Buddhist engaged in Hasidic practice will become more emotionally aware and adept. But a Jewish soul cannot be ultimately fulfilled through a Buddhist path, no more than a Buddhist can be fulfilled through the 613 *mitzvot*.

Neither can the heart wish to be the brain, nor the brain, the heart. It takes many threads of different colors to complete the beauty of the cosmic tapestry, hence the difference in meditational practice for the Jew and the non-Jew.

There are many ways to focus in meditation. Sound plays an important part, especially the sound of the letters and words that are articulated through the ladder of *tefillah* (prayer). But this requires insight on how to climb this ladder during *Shacharit, Minchah,* and *Ma'ariv* (the three set prayers of the day). There are many foci for Jewish meditation.

Also, a good focal point is music, the *niggun,* the tune in search of its own unknowable end that the masters composed to open the mind or open the heart. Others resonate with a certain moment in time—Shabbat or *Yom Tov.* And then there is also meditational dance such as the Hasidic circle that whirls and swirls.

Every *mitzvah* affords a focus for Jewish meditation. The morning affirmation of *"Modeh Ani"* transforms the moment of waking into a meaningful dynamic of ego abnegations as we become fully conscious, swing onto the side of the bed, place the right hand on top of the left, incline the head, and meditate on the essence of the *Modeh* and transform the seeming adversities into *Hashgachah*-driven opportunities.

Some of these terms and phrases may not be familiar to you. Hillel's suffix to his golden rule of "Don't do to others what you would not want done to you" was "Go and learn" the Torah.

Find a teacher. This is your personal *Nissayon* (mission) in life. It's right there in your back yard, not in the Himalayas. Now go and learn!

✳

Shohama Wiener is the President of The Academy for Jewish Religion in New York City, a pluralistic seminary ordaining rabbis and cantors. She is co-author of *Worlds of Jewish Prayer* (Jason Aronson). In this essay, Rabbi Wiener contemplates the power of meditation to heal both the meditator and the person being meditated for. She believes that the power of blessing, which is an inherent part of the Jewish tradition, is a profound meditative technique.

16 Healing and Meditation

RABBI SHOHAMA WIENER

The best-known Jewish prayer, the *Sh'ma*, is a prayer that tells us to *listen*. For me, the purpose of listening is to hear the beating heart of the universe—to know that we're all part of a realm of light where the heart sings, the eyes feel, and the hands hear. It is where souls embrace without touching and where love is the breath of life. This is what tradition says about *Gan Eden*, the Garden of Eden, a place of incredible blessing and joy, a place where everyone is healed.

Of course, that place is right here. We don't have to wait for the World to Come to experience this. We can enter it by achieving a state of altered consciousness through meditating. The sages taught that Shabbat is a taste of the World to Come. But the way most people spend Shabbat gives them such little taste of the World to Come that it is meaningless. Meditation can bring silence back into our lives, and the silence can bring a sweet awareness of the possibilities of Shabbat, the possibilities of our lives, and the reality of *Gan Eden*.

Of course, there is not ultimate silence. It's only a question of what we are listening to. Are we listening to the noises in the street? Or are we listening to what is in our heart, our mind, our body, and our soul?

MEDITATION AND HEALING

Healing is meant to make us whole. In a mystical sense, making whole combines the male and female aspects of God.

Practically though, healing works better when we try to heal others rather than ourselves. When I teach meditation, I pair people up. For one week, we meditate *for* each other, and we bless each other through prayer or visualization. We ask our partners to tell us something they very much want. Some people will say, "I've been concerned about my son" or "I have a terrible relationship with my boss." What they say doesn't matter very much. What is important is that the partner will meditate for someone else. When we do this, the heart and the spirit naturally open, and we receive blessings in the process of sending them.

ANGER, AGITATION, AND OTHER OBSTACLES

A long-term practice to cultivate is letting go of anger. A key to this is found in the prayer and meditation the Kabbalistic tradition suggests we do before reciting the bedtime *Sh'ma*: "May I forgive anyone who has harmed me, on purpose or by accident, in this lifetime or in any other lifetime." What is required is to send blessings to the people we're angry at. If you're too angry to do this, ask somebody to help you. People may say, "I've been angry at my father for twenty years. I can't let go of it. He's a beast." And I say, "Look, he's a beast because he's hurting, and this anger that you're carrying is making you ill. It is making you spiritually and emotionally ill, and if you hold onto it long enough, it will make you physically ill, too."

Making blessings and releasing anger are connected. When we bless someone, we cannot hold on to anger. When we open our heart to God's energy, anger cannot hold on.

Sometimes when people tune into what's inside them, they realize there is a lot of anger and fear. They get very uncomfortable and don't want to continue meditating. In these situations, I recommend a visualization, such as the letters of God's name or a repetitive chant that uses a phrase from the Bible over and over. We do this because where there is emotional turmoil, we want to quiet the mind rather than open it quickly. If the pain is very great, it should be let out in the presence of a strong *chevre* (group), a friend, or a therapist.

THE IMPORTANCE OF PERSISTENCE

Another obstacle to meditation is not believing it is important. Like any new habit, you must have the will and the motivation to do it properly and with some persistence. A way to begin is to set yourself a limited goal. Tell yourself, "I'm going to meditate for twenty minutes a day for one month, and I'll substitute this for something else I do." Once you become skillful at it, you can combine it with swimming or with walking or a lot of other daily activities. Now I try to cook in a meditative frame of mind, instead of simultaneously talking on the phone, chopping carrots, and planning my week.

Meditation is never an all-or-nothing thing. You can get to the meditative state even if your mind wanders ten times during the first five minutes that you meditate. Always return to the meditative thought or image.

Every area of Jewish tradition has aspects of meditative practice in it. Everything we do with pure intention and for *tikkun olam* (healing in the world) can become a high and profound blessing.

✳

Dr. Daniel C. Matt, a professor of Jewish Studies at Graduate Theological Union in Berkeley, California, and author of *God & the Big Bang: Discovering Harmony Between Science & Spirituality* (Jewish Lights) is concerned with how meditation can merge with mainstream Judaism. He also addresses some of the root assumptions underpinning meditation, namely the nature of *ayin* (nothingness), a term of vital importance, since it is an underlying concept for almost all mysticism. Yet, it is little discussed in Torah literature, primarily because of the perceived danger of the teaching.

17 Why Meditate?

DANIEL C. MATT

What is Jewish meditation? Does the meditator make it Jewish? Or is there a technique in itself that can be defined as Jewish?

There are Jewish meditative techniques. In Kabbalah, many techniques focus on Hebrew words, on names of God, on various *sefirot*. There is a technique of meditating on *ayin*, on "nothingness," which is traditionally seen as especially demanding and dangerous. It is also certainly the most open-ended of all the meditative techniques, since its goal is simply to surrender the self to the Divine Oneness, to that no-thingness that transcends all Jewish symbols. But the Hasidim and Aryeh Kaplan, a twentieth-century writer and meditation teacher, say that *ayin* is not recommended as a place to start.

MEDITATING ON *AYIN*, ON "NOTHINGNESS," AS A MEANS

I prefer to meditate on *ayin* rather than most other specific names, formulas, images, or symbols. There's something attractive to me about this, perhaps the deep immersion in a boundless Divine energy. At times, it seems to be the essence of spiritual experience, and everything else pales. But I know from my own experience and from others, too, that you can't live in the realm of *ayin*. We have to function in the world. So it's useful to have other techniques that you can use if you're stuck in a traffic jam or if you can put aside ten minutes in the morning.

The best way to get a handle on *ayin* is to compare it to Buddhism. The Buddhist concept of *sunyata* (emptiness) is similar to *ayin*—not identical, but very close.

Being born into a tradition places a demand upon us. It's useful to explore all of the spiritualities of the world, to learn from the insights of each. On the other hand, there's a natural connection we feel with the faith in which we've been raised, and that should be honored, too. Learning how to balance the particular and the universal, the Jewish and the non-Jewish, is one of the challenges on the spiritual search.

Immersion in *ayin*, though, is not the ultimate goal. Such immersion is meant to recharge our batteries. It's an immersion for the purpose of emerging, an immersion to enable us to express ourselves in a constantly "renewed form." It's useful to immerse in *ayin*, in nothingness, but it would be very bad to be stuck there, since this could easily lead to delusions or to extreme withdrawal from the daily give-and-take of life.

ENLIGHTENMENT

A permanent state of enlightenment seems to be the model in the East. Once you attain enlightenment, you never lose it or fall from it. But in the West and in Judaism, it's somewhat different. I'm not going to rule out the possibility that a Jew who is enlightened can be enlightened just as spiritual seekers are in the East. But the West and Judaism are more engaged in community and in history than is Buddhism. And the commitment to transform the mundane into the divine, to transform the "potentially" holy into the holy, is profoundly Jewish. We're engaged in the world; we cannot flee from it. Acknowledging this is a sign of the success of our meditation.

SILENCE

American Judaism profoundly needs group meditation and communal silence. This is a productive, rich kind of silence. Today, a number of rabbis are introducing this around the country, but still in a limited way. Yet, it is one of the most significant developments in contemporary Jewish spirituality.

Traditionally, parts of the worship service are silent, but words dominate, even if they are read silently. True silent meditation will help people appreciate the words. There should be fewer words and more room for silence. Then, when the words do appear, they will be more powerful. The silence will enrich the words.

Of course, a fair amount of people don't believe meditation has a place in the regular service. But there are ways to introduce meditation gradually and gently, such as a minute of pregnant silence after a *niggun,* a special wordless melody. Try this and see how the group responds.

VARIETIES OF JEWISH MEDITATION

There are different meditative techniques and traditions in the Jewish contemplative world. Traditionally, one distinction is between ecstatic Kabbalah and prophetic Kabbalah. Abraham Abulafia meditated on the Hebrew letters and on Divine names to "short-circuit" the workings of the mind. He used a technique he called "cutting the knots," which was meant to break through various mental and psychological constrictions by whirling these combinations of letters around mentally. This technique is still practiced.

Another technique is meditating on the words of the prayers with what I call "*sefirotic* correspondences." This means that certain words will resonate with certain *sefirot* (qualities of God's infinity made manifest in a finite world). In moving through a *berachah*, a blessing or a prayer, you contact the realm of the *sefirot*. This kind of meditation functions as part of the liturgy and ritual, expanding their meaning.

NOTHINGNESS IS EVERYTHING

The Western mind focuses on substance; the Eastern mind focuses on the interrelationship between everything. Nothing has independent being in and of itself. That's the basic insight of *sunyata*, whereas in Western mysticism, nothingness is still the ultimate essence. The West seems locked into the notion of substance. It may be pure Divine being, but it's also something. The East would criticize even this ultimate substance or essence and try to see through the illusion that there is any existent thing in and of itself.

You could say that these are two ways of describing an underlying reality that, presumably, is one and the same. But whereas *sunyata* is central to Buddhism, most Jews have never heard of *ayin*. Even in Kabbalah, it's talked about very rarely. In Hasidism, it's further developed, but of all the Hasidic teachings, maybe one percent is devoted to *ayin*.

Yet, *ayin* is central because it represents the moment of transition from Infinity (*Ein Sof*) to the *sefirot*. *Ayin* is how God unfolds. Creation is rooted in nothingness. There are roots for this positive sense of nothingness within Judaism. The Talmud, for example, states; "The words of Torah do not become real except for one who makes himself as if he is not." Job asks rhetorically, "Where is wisdom to be found?" The word *ayin* in this verse is a question: "Where?" But already in the Talmud, *ayin* is interpreted as a noun: "Wisdom is found in nothingness." In Kabbalah, it becomes Divine nothingness. Its roots lie in rabbinic literature, but Kabbalah expands this.

STARTING YOUR MEDITATION PRACTICE

When starting your mediation practice, the most important thing is discipline: "Make your study of Torah at a fixed time" (*Pirke Avot* 1:15). Sit for ten minutes and create openness. Moshe de Leon, composer of the Zohar, describes meditation in these words:

Thought reveals itself only through contemplating a little without content, contemplating sheer Spirit. The contemplation is imperfect. First, you understand, then you lose what you have understood. Like pondering a thought: The light of that thought suddenly darkens and vanishes. Then it returns and shines and vanishes again. No one can understand the content of that light. It is like the light that appears when water ripples in a bowl. Shining here, suddenly disappearing, then reappearing somewhere else. You think that you have grasped the light when suddenly it escapes, radiating elsewhere. You pursue it, hoping to catch it but you cannot. Yet you cannot bring yourself to leave. You keep pursuing it. It is the same with the beginning of emanation. As you begin to contemplate it, it vanishes, then reappears. You understand, then it disappears. Even though you do not grasp it, do not despair. The Source is still emanating, spreading.

Sitting for five minutes or ten minutes or even two minutes is very demanding. And to not think of anything while doing this? We can't do that. Thoughts will come, so let the thoughts come and don't hold on to them. The thought will then move on. You're then left with a gap of *ayin*, of emptiness. You contemplate just the mental process itself, without being attached to any particular idea or image or desire that pops up.

Or you can sit outdoors near a body of water and watch the light reflecting off the water. See the ephemeral nature of the mind in front of you and experience it mentally. The water itself becomes a mantra. Seeing that helps recall to you what is going on mentally.

A simpler way to start a meditation practice is just to open the siddur and find one word, one phrase, one line that's moving, uplifting, inspirational, spiritual, colorful, intriguing—and meditate on it. Start with something that attracts you in the tradition. Or take a melody, preferably one without words, or a chant, and then enter silence.

OBSTACLES TO MEDITATION

Common obstacles to meditative practices are boredom, pride, and laziness. Pride is an obstacle when you've actually made some breakthrough. You can be proud of meditating. You can be proud of being nothing.

Some *Musar* (ethical) literature can help you overcome these obstacles, as can Yitzhak Buxbaum's book, *Jewish Spiritual Practices.*

INTEGRATING MEDITATION
WITH YOUR LIFE

If I approach life with the bit of clarity that I can gain through meditation, then my life will be less secular and more spiritual. You integrate meditation and life just by being sensitive to the possibilities that arise: the possibilities of relationship, the possibilities of creativity that we often miss. Starting the day with a little bit of tranquillity can help you identify those opportunities and engage them.

One of the benefits of meditation is that it enables us to surrender the images we have of God and self. Meditation is an opportunity to melt these down and refashion them.

The Bible demands that we smash the idols. We can extend this idea from the physical idols of stone to the mental concept of God. Each smashing of an image allows for a more expanded image, which itself must be expanded until we have smashed all the images. That's what happens in the laboratory of meditation. Then we confront God anew every moment.

✳

David Cooper is director of the Heart of Stillness Retreat Center near
Boulder, Colorado. He leads intensive meditation retreats all over the
United States and has written *The Heart of Stillness, Renewing Your
Soul,* and *God Is a Verb.* Here, Rabbi Cooper points out the advantages offered by meditation and defines some of the expansion of the
possibilities of meditation that still remain to happen.

18 The Promise of Jewish Meditation

RABBI DAVID COOPER

The eternal, existential question is, "What are we doing here?
What is this all about? Is there purpose or anything beyond what
I see in front of me?" Science and technology simply don't answer the most relevant questions. Science gives us facts and
important information but doesn't speak to our hearts and to
our souls. So, there is a natural inclination for people to do what
I call contemplative practice, such as taking a walk in the woods
or staring at a slow-burning fire. These put us into a different
frame of mind, and we realize there is some other kind of reality. The next natural inclination is to formalize some of these
practices.

It's natural for us to inquire into the purpose and the reason for life. The contemplation occurs when we make an effort
to do things that are a little bit different from the normal flow
of life, such as being quiet or secluding ourselves, for the mys-

tical realm doesn't lend itself to anything other than contemplative inquiry, and it surely cannot be scientifically analyzed.

Since meditation can be seen as multiple forms of inquiry, most people can find a form of inquiry that suits them. For example, certain kinds of yoga appeal to intellectual inquiry, while karma yoga appeals to a more physically involved person. Different kinds of meditative techniques will be more beneficial for certain types of personalities and types of people. There are different forms for different people, but some general things really apply to everybody. Shabbat is an example. Shabbat is an exercise in managing time and giving ourselves time. How we work with our Shabbat time is affected by who we are, what kind of a person we are, and what kind of a meditator we want to be. Everyone can benefit from this.

But for many people, Shabbat is unthinkable because it eats up too much of their time. This, of course, is the very syndrome that Shabbat struggles with: how to work with time. So the misunderstanding arises that by taking a day off, it will add to our time burden because we need to use, as "fully" as we can, every moment of our day. Ironically, by taking time off, we manage our time for the rest of the week better. But we don't have that clarity unless we create a space for some kind of time for reflection. India, for example, is very different from the United States, and Indians have a totally different relationship to time. Anybody who travels there instantly encounters this relationship. Here, we get on an airplane that leaves at a specific minute and arrives almost at the exact minute that it's supposed to. There, we think a train is going to arrive at the station at a certain time, and it might not come until the next day. This relationship to time very quickly changes our expectations.

The Jewish notion of time is somewhere in between. It says

that there are six days—and then there is Shabbat. So, the six days we put into a time and space frame, and Shabbat becomes conceptually exclusive of time and space. This is a wonderful understanding of time because it really says that the time between Sunday and Friday is the time of the mundane world. But when sundown on Friday arrives, we can forget about time, and we shouldn't think about our workweek. We are in Shabbat, in a different state of time, in a different reality. Jewish mysticism is built on the relativity of time. There is neither time nor space in the soul realms and no time in the angelic realms. There is no past and no future.

PERSONAL REVELATION AND COLLECTIVE REVELATION

Every spiritual tradition has been built experientially on some kind of personal experience with the Divine. Religious traditions are not built on *intellectual* revelation. They're built on something that happens in the *kishkes* (gut). And so, I have to assume that any faith—Judaism or Islam or Buddhism—is based on a personal revelation that profoundly changed someone's life. Judaism describes these great revelations; each of us was at Mount Sinai and came out of Egypt. We describe these not just as stories but project ourselves into their space and time and realize that they are a profound connecting point with the Divine.

Mainstream Judaism today has become distanced from the substance of the experience. This means that if practitioners go in and work with ritual as form, rather than as substance, it won't take long for them to feel separated from what they're doing because it's not a fully integrated experience. They're just working with form. And they will stop because if there's no experience that touches their *kishkes,* then nothing will nurture their soul.

Think of meditation as any kind of activity that brings us closer to the experience of what's really happening *here.* Mainstream Judaism must bring technique (we'll call it "meditation") to do this. I'm not talking about just sitting, crossing your legs, and looking at your navel type of meditation. I'm saying it has to be inclusive and raise awareness. Mainstream Judaism *must* have this to survive. It is happening in little bits and pieces, but there is not much of it. A great example: Sitting in yeshiva and learning was a profound meditative experience for me. The yeshiva *bocher,* or student, learns from morning until night and comes out with an altered frame of consciousness. This is a very strong meditative practice, but there is no emphasis on the psychology of what they're doing or acknowledgment and honoring of the process that's taking place. Instead of utilizing this altered state of consciousness that one attains and the exquisite, shared consciousness that moves the student, there is just a rush to do the prayers just so and a rush to get more and more and more knowledge. It becomes neurotic. So we need to change our frame of reference.

The very religious world is extremely contemplative without knowing it. But mainstream Jews don't have a strong daily practice, and this is a serious problem. They are very, very busy in their daily lives and use Judaism almost solely as *form*: Here comes *Pesach,* so let's have a Seder. They read the Haggadah in 45 minutes, and every word that is supposed to be said is said and then it's time to eat.

Or, here comes Rosh Hashanah: They pay a lot of money for synagogue seats, to hear the shofar (ram's horn), to do everything they are supposed to do. This is almost tragic because hearing the shofar without completely surrendering to its call doesn't fulfill the *mitzvah* (commandment), not in the deepest realm. These are the Jews I am most concerned about. Not those who have completely fallen away. Not the ones who are completely immersed in their practice. But the big, middle core of Judaism that yearns to connect with meaning and purpose.

JEWISH ENERGY, JEWISH TRADITION

In the last few years, there has been more interest in meditation and more willingness to explore Judaism in a way that is somewhat atypical from the kind of exploration that people did even a decade ago. For example, silent retreats of seven to ten days that I lead are becoming more and more successful in terms of the numbers of people who attend. And I find that people today realize that talking and a busy mind don't have to be associated with Jewish practice.

Jewish meditation is starting to come out of the closet. Anyone who is a serious spiritual seeker (and I put every rabbi in that category, even though he or she may not know it) does a practice that somehow connects them. More and more rabbis come to my retreats or call to ask questions. More and more, the rabbinic world appreciates that people need some kind of contemplative activity in their spiritual lives.

Judaism is a way of life, a way of seeing things, a way of *doing* things. Eating ham and cheese would not typically fit into the Jewish way of life. But it doesn't necessarily exclude somebody from being Jewish. This brings us to a question: Do I have to eat in a certain way in order to be Jewish? Can I be Jewish if I eat anything I want? This is one of these wonderful issues for which there is no final answer. For me, Judaism has to do with our connection to the Divine. And it also has to do with an energy that has been introduced over thousands of years. For example, there is some debate today over whether a newborn boy should be circumcised. For thousands of years, Judaism has been saying that an eight-day-old child is circumcised and is then, by definition, Jewish. And I feel that certain aspects of our tradition have so much energy built into them that they cannot be denied.

For me, Judaism has to do with connecting mystically to a path that millions of people have walked for thousands of years. How that expresses itself we can debate, but Jewish meditation somehow fits into this path and guides us to it and along it. The question of how to begin a Jewish meditation practice is attached to where persons hold themselves Jewishly before they begin. Say somebody comes to me who's not Jewish and is really interested in practicing the kabbalistic names of God. I say, "I'll teach you this meditative practice, but if you're going to church on Sunday and you have an intimate relationship with Jesus, I want you to know that what I'm teaching is a concentration practice developed in a Jewish model." I will not call it Jewish meditation practice because it only becomes that if you're looking at life Jewishly. We now have some people in the Buddhist world, and even a few Buddhist teachers, who practice these methods.

JEWISH CONTEMPLATIVE PRACTICE— STARTING WITH SIMPLE THINGS

If individuals really want to deepen their relationship to Judaism and ask me what kind of Jewish contemplative practice they can do, we start with Shabbat. We examine what they already do on this one day and discuss several awareness building exercises they can do. I start with very fundamental things, such as a contemplative form of meditation in which we take a few lines of Torah and think about it for twenty minutes.

I would suggest many simple things like this before I introduce more esoteric kinds of meditation. There's a misunderstanding that the more exotic the practice, somehow the higher it's going to take us on some artificial hierarchy of awareness. This is simply not true. The simplest practices are often the most profound. In many traditions, simple things such as how we breathe and how aware we are of our breath are the most basic and, at the same time, the most advanced practice that is done. The most common obstacle today to meditation is the environment in which we live. It's extremely seductive. There's a lot of information. Television always beckons to us. People usually flip on the radio in their cars. We read newspapers and magazines and books and go to the movies. There's nothing wrong with this. But when it piles up and we are completely overwhelmed, it all becomes a burden, and the most important part of life—the spiritual—is ignored. The only way we can reprioritize our lives is to understand what it means to live such a busy life. One of the greatest teachings of our tradition is that the greatest gift we can be given precedes being released from enslavement. And the greatest gift is to *recognize* that we are slaves. If we don't know that we are enslaved, then we just continue being slaves. Our tradition teaches that eighty percent of the people in Egypt didn't recognize that they were enslaved and stayed in slavery. I realize that the only way to achieve freedom is to *get out* of this constricted place and move to the next step. So, we have to understand how life today enslaves us, and then we need techniques that can help us. Once we see our enslavement, then our priorities will change, and we won't let our busy life dominate us. At that point, we have the opportunity to make some deep personal changes in how we live and to develop some spiritual practices that bring some balance to our lives.

✳

Andrea Cohen-Kiener is an educator and meditation teacher. Her book *Conscious Community: A Guide to Inner Work* discusses, as does this teaching, some of the possibilities inherent in meditation. Cohen-Kiener is interested in creating a model for life, through meditation, that can be utilized and sustained by large numbers of individuals.

---

19 Go to Your Self

ANDREA COHEN-KIENER

Judaism offers a very good "Travel Guide to Life in the Universe." It provides information on the destination, the purpose of the journey, where to eat along the way, good sites to visit as we travel, and so on. All these aspects are important. Judaism places us in a very meaningful position in a glorious and complex universe. It provides us with a Way.

Some dimensions of the Jewish way are better known than others. Judaism has unique prayers and an annual liturgical cycle. Jews have well-defined laws and customs and practice a good part of their faith in community, which is textually based and has a deep love of learning. They have developed many layers of religious literature and many ways of probing beloved texts. Less well-known are the dimensions of Judaism that illuminate a theory of the human personality, such as the *Musar* and Hasidic counseling models and mysticism and philosophy. These are the areas in which meditation will help us the most. So we need to say a little bit about the structure of the universe and the potential of the human persona.

References to altered states of consciousness (and the practices that help us achieve them) are in Torah and the literature about it, but you need to be aware of the spiritual process to recognize them. Much Jewish tradition was received by prophets who had prepared themselves to be sensitive to *ruach hakodesh*, or "divine inspiration." We have references to certain body postures that are similar to the *asanas*, or "postures," of yoga, favored by Elijah the Prophet (according to the tradition). The priests in the Temple proscribed movements as well as chants to facilitate their *avodat hakodesh,* or "spiritual work." Samuel the Prophet used music to achieve trance states. Mystical states generated when people were in groups were so powerful that the young warrior Saul was once swept up into such a state and began to sing and dance with the "sons of the prophets."

The events at Sinai may be looked at this way: Six hundred thousand adults prepared for three days at the foot of a mountain to receive Torah. Moses, himself, spent forty days on top of Sinai. His experience parallels the founding moments of many traditions, including Judaism. Whatever our opinion may be about the process of revelation, if six hundred thousand people meditate for three days in a desert, they will arrive at a deeper understanding of the Divine.

THE RECOVERY OF JEWISH ESOTERICISM

The transmission of Jewish consciousness work continued through every phase of our history and every level of our literature. It evolved as we came into contact with many other cultures. Each century and locale had its own special flavor of spirit that grew up under the influence of the paradigm of its time and its special teachers. There were especially profound and rapid developments in spiritual transmission in thirteenth-century Poland, fifteenth-century Iberia, sixteenth-century Safed, and eighteenth-century Poland.

How did these Jewish teachings become virtually lost in our generation? The question has many answers. Historically, there were many ruptures in the fabric of Jewish life. Most recently, the Holocaust snuffed out a huge percentage of Jewish esoteric teachers (in a largely oral tradition) in one decade. Many Jews who left Poland and Russia before each of the two world wars were not especially pious and spiritual; they were adventurous and discontent with their secular lives. So the new Jews in America were not particularly oriented toward meditation and working on their mindfulness. It took the materialistic gorging of the 1950s and the social disaffections of the 1960s to awaken a new generation of Jewish souls to this work. By then, the trail of Jewish meditation was pretty cold. Most of my peers who meditate learned to do so from Sufis, Hindus, and Buddhists. Few learned from Jewish texts or from living Jewish teachers.

Other factors also worked against the vibrant transmission of a Jewish spirituality. The majority of American Jews go through most of their formal religious education before the age of thirteen. Even if one's teacher is spiritually sensitive, the young student usually wants recess more than deep spiritual work. So, as a more or less spiritually disaffected adult, it becomes truly hard to find ways to raise your level of Jewish observance (which is statistically likely to be flaccid) and to satisfy your thirst for spiritual teachings, which is likely to be quite urgent and profound.

Enter Reb Zalman Schachter-Shalomi, Reb Shlomo Carlebach z"l, Rabbi Dovid Din, Reb Meir Fund, and many other blessed and daring souls who helped an entire generation of Jews synthesize the eclectic learnings of our "seeker years" with Jewish practice and teaching. I heard a teaching once by Reb Shlomo z"l, that the Holy One has some purpose in mixing the spiritual pot so deeply now that Jews are learning with Moslems and Hindus and pagans and Buddhists and Native Americans and Catholics: when we give and take with other sensitive souls on the planet, we reclaim some pieces of a living tradition that has reached us in a somewhat tattered condition.

So we blend hints and pieces of the Jewish meditation tradition with the experience of being at, say, an ashram or a Wild Woman retreat. But before we can understand how meditation can be used in our Jewish practice, we need to learn more about the universe and comprehend more astutely the Jewish system of being.

JOURNEYING THROUGH THE FOUR WORLDS

One key conceptual framework for Jewish cosmology and personality theory has been widely disseminated since refugees from the Spanish expulsion established a spiritual center in Safed in northern Israel in the sixteenth century. Their mental picture of the universe— *torat arba olamot*, or the Doctrine of the Four Worlds—parallels many other world traditions and is the foundation for a good definition of spiritual practice. It maintains that everything in creation moves from the most subtle to the more manifest and concrete. The structure of humans holds the pattern of the Four Worlds: Inspiration, Thought, Affect, and Action.

The most subtle of the four realms is *Atzilut*, which means "will." The motivation for the creation of the universe arose as a moment of will in the Divine mind. We cannot say much about this because our limited language and concepts prevent us from describing it well. But since we are created in the Divine image, we can see for ourselves that inspiration, guidance, or will must precede new effort.

The next world is the world of *Briyah*, of "conceptualization." This is the realm of ideas, of blueprints. Of this level, we say, "*Sof maaseh b'machshava techillah*," "Anything that comes to be, starts as an idea." With *Briyah*, the unfolding of the universe now enters the planning stages. At our concrete, physical level of life, inspiration and planning are how we begin action and how we create.

Next is *Yetzirah*, which means "formula" or "creativity." In the human experience, this is the emotional realm. The interface between us and God happens here. God manifests Truth, Love, Balance, Permanence, Glory and Strength—and we reach for them. Clearing our emotional channels to reach for the One is how we enter the world of *Yetzirah*, the world of longing.

The final world is called *Asiyah*, which roughly means "just do it." This describes the physical properties of the world around us.

Upon reaching *Asiyah*, each "world" interpenetrates with one other. Each realm, one no less than another, reflects the Divine will and is a witness to Unity. However, since we do live in *Asiyah*—a world of apparent distinctions and opposites, of disparity and separation—our separateness is more obvious than our unity. Yet, we are the people who say *Adonai Echad*, God is One. Here, in the physical world, it is an act of faith to remember the One.

Let's look at another manifestation of this theory. The human body reflects the attributes of each "world" and how they manifest in us. The Jewish esoteric tradition teaches that *Asiyah* is energized through our lower body. From the liver down, we are divided and polarized (through our two legs); we make contact with the earth; we reproduce physically.

Yetzirah, or "feeling," operates through the human torso and, specifically, the heart. The heart, which gives and receives, needs to be flexible yet firm so it can open channels to do its work. It carries fluid to every part of the body, but the farther a part of the body is from its center (the heart), the more fragmentary is the delivery system (blood vessels). So, too, are emotions fluid. Sometimes, we feel as though we will be swept away if we open the door to feeling. In the symbolic language of Torah, water often refers to deep feeling. It is at wells where our Patriarchs meet their *bashert* (cosmically ordained marriage partners). It is at the crossing of seas where we make final transitions.

The world of *Briyah* manifests in our neural system. The mind lets us compare, calculate, recall, infer, and imagine; it also has many capacities which we have yet to fully develop. *Briyah* may be the most pliable of the three lower worlds. Intuition, directed attention, blessing, telepathy, and other skills involve concentrated use of the mind, abilities that most people can develop to some degree. One of the benefits of meditation is being able to better watch and direct what our minds do and how they work.

We have progressed through the human body from the legs to the head, yet we have one world left to find: *Atzilut*, or "nearness." This fourth realm, which is something like our soul root, is too big to fit into the body. In Hasidic language, the soul wears the "protective suit" called the "body" so it can operate in the harsh environment of *Asiyah*. The soul energizes the body and hovers above and around it, as it were. We are as open to the presence of the soul as our level of consciousness allows.

How we give, receive, nourish, process, and grow is different in each of the Four Worlds. This is not an esoteric concept. We all know when we are "stuck in our heads" or "carrying tension in our bodies" or "completely emotional." The simple cosmology of the Four Worlds provides a framework for viewing our activity and our motives. Meditation can help us get a handle, a vantage point, from which to watch ourselves so we can be more aware about how we react to things. Then we can be more deliberate in how we choose to act.

USING TORAH AS OUR GUIDE

Now that we have a schematic of the Jewish world-view, we can settle on a definition of spirituality: When our doing, feeling, and understanding (the lower three realms) are all doing the same thing, we are having a spiritual experience. And the way to open ourselves to *Atzilut* or "spirit" is to make a vessel for the Divine from our lower three capacities.

How does this work? If I am an observant Jew and I eat an apple, I recite a blessing beforehand. I bless in the world of *Asiyah*. I may experience a moment of smugness ("Aha, I remember to bless!"), but I have not really had a spiritual experience. I have not really elevated myself or the act of eating. But now let us say that I remember to open in the heart: I open an emotional connection to the act. I am truly appreciative of the apple. I am hungry, and it is sweet and delicious. I add to my blessing some quality from *Yetzirah*, or "affect," so that after saying a blessing, I am moved. I am then nourished by eating the apple in two worlds. Now let us add a third world. In Chabad Hasidism, there is a widely quoted saying: "The Holy One takes spiritual essence and makes a concrete world of it." Human beings do just the opposite, using physical objects to reveal their spiritual root. Thus, we turn materiality back into spirit. In the moment of blessing, I pause to rein in my physical appetite. I experience my gratefulness for the food and know that I am part of the upper worlds. That's a blessing and an eating that changes us.

But simply watching ourselves through the prism of the Four Worlds is useful, but unguided. We must align ourselves in all Four Worlds with the wisdom of Torah. Let's take the example of *shmirat halashon*, or "right speech." The thumbnail rule is that we are not allowed to say anything negative about anybody else unless we are speaking directly to them with the purpose of helping each other, or our mutual evolution, or to prevent them from causing further harm to themselves or to others. I can observe that law in *Asiyah*: shutting my mouth and not saying what I am bursting to say. Often when I am bursting with this negativity, it's because I feel slighted. But how do I feel slighted? Why do I care about this person's attention? These are fundamental questions to work through. We can follow the example into *Briyah*: We learn in *Tomer Devorah* (a mystically inspired tract on personality traits written by Rabbi Moses Cordovero in the sixteenth century) that our craving to be seen and recognized has a parallel in God, who sustains every being at every moment and is virtually ignored and constantly underappreciated by the recipients of His mercy. If we can recognize our Creator and feel the mutual love that flows between us, we will yearn less for the approval and attention of others.

Using the Four Worlds model, we can watch our impulses and align ourselves with more noble characteristics.

The unique position of each person is that we all have unique opportunities to consciously bring godliness into the physical realm. Jewish practices of talking, eating, waking up in the morning, dressing, praying, farming, taxing, even walking through a doorway can be described as balancing acts that let us simultaneously enjoy our physical pleasures and be mindful of God. They let us join the highest worlds with the lower worlds. *With this consciousness, our every act becomes a meditation.*

OPENING OUR MINDS

Mindfulness meditation is a precursor to all inner work, including Four Worlds Judaism. Mindfulness itself is a universal practice of developing a better capacity to be aware of oneself. Thich Nhat Hanh, a Vietnamese Buddhist, is probably the best known proponent of this practice today. But several Jewish teachers also transmitted a form of mindfulness meditation, especially Reb Kalonymos Kalmish Shapira in Warsaw before and during World War II.

Mindfulness meditation sounds deceptively simple. Let's say you have decided to sit quietly for twenty minutes and watch your breath. In a nanosecond, your mind will begin anticipating the day's activities or think about writing a long letter or drawing up shopping lists. After a few more seconds, you will notice that this has happened ("Darn, I'm not meditating"), and you will return to again watching your breath for another several nanoseconds before you drift off again. As you pull your attention back to task, you are building a muscle that will be with you after the meditation. This has enormous benefits for daily life. Later that day, as you watch yourself get pulled off task again, you can taste it faster because you spent some time earlier that day being deeply centered. In the very moment of watching yourself go off center, you sense a freedom of choice: you can go there or not. Seeing the choice is the only way to have that freedom. Meditation helps us practice that.

When you first noticed that you weren't watching your breath, you may have said, "I can't even sit quietly..." You beat yourself up. Don't worry about this, we all do this a lot. Meditation, which is an internal slowing and watching, helps us amplify that inner dialogue. But once we see, we have a choice. I can beat myself up for getting lost in a thought strand or for being arrogant or fearful, or I can calmly return to task. Getting a handle on inner dialogue, on our little self-sabotaging inner messages, is another powerful benefit of meditation.

Guided meditation can also have very rich Jewish applications. This meditation is perhaps the most popular form of meditation. It is used by gym teachers, the National Cancer Institute, and busy executives. But guided meditation that draws us into the symbols of Judaism is a Jewish meditation. The symbolism of the *sefirot* system, the Hebrew alphabet, biblical phrases, and key moments in the Patriarchal narrative can open us to endless levels of meaning if we use them as objects for meditation.

Hasidism calls this *Hitbonenut*, which derives from a Hebrew root meaning "build" and "discern." I usually translate *Hitbonenut* as "long thinking," which means that we sit with a text (or a word or a letter) and open ourselves to its layers of meaning. If we study a Hebrew text this way, we might look at the Exodus story and ask, "Why did a lamb have to die? What does the symbolism of sacrifice mean?" We find the riddles implicit in the text, and we personalize them. We enter the story of the text—and the story enters us. Whatever our level of consciousness, we all need to deepen our knowing of Judaism so its rich heritage can enrich our inner work. Take yourself seriously but not too seriously. Trust your intuition. If you are sincere and if you continue to learn more about Judaism, you'll find new depth in your Jewish practice and your meditation practice.

The Mishnah teaches that you need to get a teacher and gain a study partner. When we begin our journey inward, we encounter psychic wounds that need healing. The journey takes courage. That is why the Holy One didn't put us here alone. A valued friend can help us with our inner cleansing.

The Jewish story begins with a journey: the journey of Abraham. His journey began with the words "*Lech lecha*," "Get going." The Hebrew carries another possible translation: "Go. Go to your Self."

✳

Lynn Gottleib was the first woman ordained as a Jewish Renewal rabbi. She received her ordination from The Jewish Theological Seminary and co-founded Congregation Nahalaat Shalom in Albuquerque, New Mexico, where she continues to serve as spiritual leader. Rabbi Gottleib is active in reinvigorating Jewish liturgy and theology to include women's Torah. Her teaching points out that meditation must include this vital component, a component of profound innovation and rethinking traditional wisdom to include women's wisdom. Doing so will stretch the very idea of what meditation is.

---

20 Meditation and Women's Kabbalah

RABBI LYNN GOTTLEIB

Ideally, Jewish religious practice is dedicated to honoring life and to deepening our capacity for compassion. As the present generation of Jews attempts to reconnect their longing for spiritual existence to sources of spirituality within Jewish culture, many have returned to prayerful practices within our tradition's vast storehouses of wisdom. This has generated a renewed interest in Kabbalah, a part of Jewish tradition devoted to cultivating wholeness of being.

Kabbalah is home to many systems of belief about the nature of existence. These systems reflect the times they come from just as much as they may reflect eternal truths about the nature of human consciousness. Kabbalah has integrated aspects of Greek science and philosophy, medieval alchemy, Sufi reverence for mystical language, and contemporary psychology, physics, and feminism into its theological ideas and mystical practices. Kabbalah can be seen as an ongoing Jewish meditation on the question of how we manifest the sacred in daily life.

Since human consciousness is affected by social and cultural assumptions, what is considered true in one era can be deconstructed in the next. What is elevated as a path toward wholeness by one generation can be seen as oppressive by a subsequent generation. Patterns of awareness are relative. Perhaps to save ourselves from confusion, we pretend we know things. Therefore, a measure of the worth of any kabbalistic teaching should relate to the well-being of real individuals and be useful to the spiritual task of fostering compassion, wholeness of being, creativity, and joy. With these thoughts, I come to the question of how Kabbalah and traditional Jewish meditation techniques relate to contemporary Jewish women's lives.

LETTING WOMEN'S SPIRITUALITY INTO THE TRADITION

As we now know, Jewish culture delineated the scope of women's and men's activities on the basis of gender definition and created physical and spiritual boundaries separating them. That boundary often prevented women from engaging in the study and creation of Torah, leading public prayer, and conducting such home ceremonies as the Seder. One of the dominant symbols of that separation is the *mehitzah*, the partition found in what are now called "Orthodox" synagogues. Women sit behind a screen or on a balcony in a room that often has a separate entrance from the one used by men. Women have been and still are second-class citizens of the Jewish communal polity. While both men and women participated in the creation and sustenance of Jewish life and culture, women's religious traditions cultivated on their side of the partition were not considered official "text" by their male counterparts. Women were not part of kabbalistic study or prayer groups (with a few rare exceptions). From our contemporary perspective, we can say that male authors of the Kabbalah may have related to Jewish women's material well-being or even to their happiness. They have even respected the piety of certain women. But women were not part of kabbalistic conversations. The formation of Kabbalah seems to have taken place almost entirely on the men's side of the *mehitzah*. Thus, to speak of Jewish meditation or the Kabbalah as the primary source for Jewish spiritual practices is to exclude women's spiritual experience and women's diverse expressions of sacred consciousness from the process of Jewish renewal.

There is another challenge for feminist women and men in the study and application of Kabbalah as a source for contemporary Jewish practice. Even though the Kabbalah is a diverse tradition with many voices over centuries, the one element that these diverse expressions share is the idea that archetypal female energy is both passive and in need of redemption by an active male potency—and that it is dangerous or demonic when not under control by its male counterpart. The feminine is also the site for conversations about the nature of evil, seduction, impiety, impurity, materiality, and abuse. Whenever Jewish tradition wants to highlight suffering, it is often the image of a raped or abandoned woman. This attitude about feminine nature and potencies corresponds to Jewish culture's ambivalence about women's assertiveness and creativity. The loudness of her voice, the expression of her sexuality, the development of her intellect, and her use of charismatic or spiritual powers has evoked fear and disgust more than admiration and support. Jewish sacred narratives that promote a view of feminine energy as a secondary, inferior, or evil presence must undergo change so they can truly be vessels of liberation and compassion for women as well as men.

"WOMEN'S KABBALAH"

However, redesigning existing male texts is not enough. Even as we reconstruct Jewish theology from feminist perspectives, let us not forget to turn to women's sources of religious thought and practice. Contemporary scholars in the field of Jewish women's studies such as Gerda Lerner, Judith Plaskow, Susan Starr Sered, and many others have documented and analyzed Jewish women's history. They have begun the process of restoring women to the narrative of Jewish women's history and begun restoring women to the narrative of Jewish memory. From the days of the midwives of Israel to the contemporary period, Jewish women have developed lasting traditions of herbal remedies, sacred dance, amulets, drumming, healing hands, curing with fire, storytelling, meditation, prayer, and advice-giving techniques, as well as the creation of ritual customs for each Jewish festival and life-cycle occasion. We might even speak of these practices as "women's Kabbalah" because they are spiritual traditions handed down from generation to generation by wise women in each community.

Unfortunately, women's religious practices have often been associated with idolatry or regarded as illegitimate and unworthy of serious consideration. Many women, however, are drawn to look precisely in the places regarded as taboo by conventional authorities because that is where our creativity and positive power can often be found. At a recent class about the Sephardic Jews of New Mexico, I was awakened, once again, to the remembrance of Jewish women's spiritual traditions as a living reality—as institutions of spiritual transformation and physical healing.

Emma Montoya, a New Mexican *cuandera* (healer), smiled at her cousin, removed an herb from a plastic pouch, and began to highlight its medicinal qualities. She was teaching this week's class at a local synagogue about the Sephardic Jews of New Mexico. Emma informed us that Jewish women midwives and doctors practiced medicine in medieval Spain. They could be found in the service of royalty, and some even obtained authorization to practice medicine from the king himself. When they fled the Inquisition, many Sephardic families brought their healing traditions to the New World, where they combined traditional medical knowledge with acquired learning about the plants growing in their new environment. Emma is heir to hundreds of years of her family's Sephardic medicinal and spiritual wisdom. She has listened to her elders, read through extensive family medical journals, practiced her medicine on herself, and learned the songs of praise that she chants whenever she prepares and administers her remedies. At births and deaths, coming of age ceremonies and marriages, she guides body and soul through another passage. During the class, she displayed some of her herbs, chanted the songs associated with them, and instructed us always to keep the doors of forgiveness open. Emma preserves and renews through her own practice an accumulated wisdom about healing and wholeness that incorporates not only spiritual guidance but also practical knowledge of remedies of a wide range of medical problems. Her knowledge is deeply intertwined with the religious practice and mystical beliefs she carries from her Sephardic and New Mexican roots. Emma's class reminds me not to forget to turn to Jewish women's wisdom. This wisdom has a relationship to the body, to the earth, to a sense of balance in the walk from life to death.

AN INNOVATIVE, INCLUSIVE
MEDITATION PRACTICE

In the spirit of these reflections, I would like to offer a meditation practice that flows from both women's and men's Jewish cultural traditions. When I decided to write a piece for this book, I began thinking of my friend Pamela Midell, a Buddhist priest who devotes her life to nuclear disarmament. She organized "The Atomic Mirror Pilgrimage" for the fiftieth year since the use of atomic bombs. About twenty of us traveled the path of the bomb from Trinity Test Site in New Mexico to Japan. At each site, I was asked to conduct a ceremony that would honor the traditions of all participants and provide a ritual occasion for each person to give witness. While on our journey, Pamela observed that storytelling is my spiritual practice, just as sitting meditation is hers. The soundness of her comment immediately struck home. Storytelling is a place in Judaism where I have been able to blend traditional male and female sources of wisdom. The Breslover Hasidim say that the Baal Shem Tov, by telling a story, was able to cause spiritual unification. When he saw that spiritual channels were blocked and he could not repair them with prayers, he would repair them with a story. Storytelling has also been a way for me to open healing channels, repair broken hearts, and provoke wonder and joy. Reb Nachman of Breslov said that if you want to understand the *Shechinah* (the all-encompassing, feminine aspect of God), go to the place women tell stories. I find myself in accord with his advice and wonder how many of his stories he adapted from women's tales.

I grew up with storytelling in the home. My mother taught creative dramatics and performed as a puppeteer to adult and children's audiences. We children would often hear my mother's pantheon of voices from the basement and leave our own play to watch her magical world. My mother's stories opened my eyes to adventurous heroines that I never would have encountered otherwise. She sometimes performed at my family's Reform temple and is the only adult woman I remember ever standing before the whole community to present her creative work.

I have been telling stories before audiences since the age of seven, when I landed my first role as the knave that stole the queen's tarts at the Civic Little Theater in Allentown, Pennsylvania. Since then I have found that storytelling is a wise teacher, a beloved friend, and a portal to the heart and mind of everyone I encounter. I have also found stories to be where I can learn about the lives of Jewish women throughout the ages. Women have actively shaped the fabulous fables and folk tales, the proverbs and practical advice, and the music and dance repertoire of every generation.

A MEDITATION TO EVOKE STORIES OF BIBLICAL WOMEN

Telling a story can be compared to building a home or sacred lodge for the imagination. This lodge is a place of giving witness to one's truth, of opening one's voice and body, of surrendering to the story's own transcendent wisdom. To enter the lodge, one must only offer a willing heart.

Jewish women's Kabbalah begins with the tradition of biblical oracle women who were considered mediums of the sacred in their time. Ancient Israel had many names for women who were spiritual leaders, such as *Devorah*, *Eshet Lapidot*, and *Em Yisrael*. I translate these as Oracle Woman, Keeper of Sacred Fires, and Clan Mother. These women often performed their work under sacred trees planted at the entrance of sacred space. Women also prophesied, healed with herbs, told stories to their families and communities, sang songs at life-cycle ceremonies, and created narratives about their experience of the world. Let us now assume the mantle of the teller, of one who gives voice to dreaming, who interprets the world around and the world within. Let us enter a storyteller's meditation, immerse ourselves in the waters of our imagination, and give way to the story that dwells inside our true heart song. And then, let us embody that story in physical retelling.

The task of this meditation is to focus on the meaning that a particular biblical character has in your life and to explore this meaning through the act of telling the story. Rather than trying to tell an entire story, we will focus on a story fragment, the piece of the story that comes to you through a guided meditation.

To prepare yourself for this meditation, pick a quiet, inspiring place: the woods behind your house, an area of your room you have set aside for your personal sacred space or praying station, the sanctuary of your synagogue.

When preparing for a meditation, I use the imagery of the *mishkan*, the Sacred Lodge. In the east side of the *mishkan* sits the incense altar. This part of the ritual is dedicated to stating your intention to seek vision, grace, wisdom, and peace. I light some dried sagebrush and juniper in a pottery bowl and make a beginning prayer as the smoke rises:

> "*Yehoyah* Spirit, I seek your vision.
> *Yehoyah* Spirit, I seek your grace.
> *Yehoyah* Spirit, I seek your wisdom.
> *Yehoyah* Spirit, I seek your peace."

After finishing this chant, I say, "This is the ceremony for the east. May my prayers rise like this sweet smoke and be a sacred offering to the fullness and compassion of life."

In the south of the *mishkan* stands the menorah, another symbol of wholeness of being. The menorah is the tree of life, representing earth, root, trunk, branch, flower, fruit, and sky.

We use our breath to open our being. Adopt a breath and movement practice for this part of the meditation. Now concentrate on using sound as you work with voice, breath, and movement. The storytelling body breaks through surface response to a deeper level. Once you feel open and relaxed, take a deep breath, sit down, and say, "This is the ceremony for the south. May my breath and movement be a sacred offering to the fullness and compassion of life."

In the west stand stones, which represent wisdom: ark and guardian spirits. In the west, we seek a vision and a story, for this is the traditional direction of wisdom. As you face the western direction of your sacred space, close your eyes and imagine you are standing somewhere in the biblical landscape. You see a biblical woman. She may be drawing water at a well, sitting by her tent, teaching at the city gates, making an offering at the Temple, serving customers at her inn, or praying in the hills.

She sees you approaching and beckons to you to come. She tells you something. You take a breath as you absorb what she tells you about her life.

When your meditation is complete, open your eyes and write down what you saw and what this biblical woman told you. What teaching did she give you?

Now say, "This is the ceremony of the west. May my meditation be a sacred offering to the fullness and compassion of life."

In the north sits a golden table laden with twelve breads, one for each of the twelve tribes of Israel. (Some Jewish women speak of thirteen as the full tribal number in order to represent the tribe of Dinah. There is also a legend that each of the twelve brothers was matched by a twin sister.) The north is where our wisdom rises and becomes a source of nourishment, not only for ourselves but also for others. Take the biblical image that appeared in your meditation and translate it into a story. Find a voice, a body, and a movement for the character through which you can become the character in your meditation.

At a workshop I presented at the Jewish Community Center in Boston, a woman saw the prophet Miriam with her drum in hand, leading the people through the Red Sea. Miriam told this woman, "Give yourself over to the dance." After we all shared our individual meditations, each woman turned her story fragment into a performance form. This woman created a dance for Miriam that expressed her fears about letting go, then used Miriam's dance as a way to let go. In the discussion that followed the performance, she told how her shyness usually inhibited her from partaking in certain experiences. After the meditation, this woman felt she "learned how to be freer with herself, like the prophet Miriam, and express her own joy and enthusiasm."

In the last section of the ritual meditation, each person becomes the storyteller and learns that the physical act of telling reveals layers of insight not available through study and discussion. We then learn more about ourselves as we move our vision into performance mode. By performing the fragment of our story, we can observe our performance choices, analyze and reflect upon them, and more deeply understand what the story might mean to us and what the story reveals about us. By focusing on the inner meaning of the story in our own lives, we have entered a realm of Kabbalah that can speak to both men and women.

✳

Dr. **Shaul Magid** teaches at the Jewish Theological Seminary in New York City. He is concerned with giving Jewish meditation a firm foundation in the tradition and combining it with other aspects of ritual observance. But he is also concerned that *halachah* be viewed as a potentially liberating rather than a limiting force in religious life. Toward this end, his idea of *halachah* as art is very intriguing, and his concept of the role of meditation in living a life of piety is challenging.

21 Piety Before Ecstasy

SHAUL MAGID

The theological and cultural debate among contemporary Jews over the validity of practicing meditation and contemplation has largely run its course. The initial trepidation among traditional and nontraditional Jewish leaders has largely proved to be unjustified, since various meditative techniques in Jewish prayer and ritual observance have reinvigorated, not diminished, the vibrancy of Jewish life. In many ways, the popularization of Jewish meditation has resulted in an unlikely link between the Jewish community and the Jewish seminaries and universities. Jewish scholars have determined the extent to which the contemplative and meditative life has played an important role in the Jewish spiritual journey. Many of these scholars have uncharacteristically disseminated their research to those who can develop and reformulate subtle, often opaque academic research into practical methods for the Jewish community.

However, many significant issues remain unresolved, and new problems continue to emerge. Particularly, there are fundamental problems in the proliferation of Jewish meditative practices that temper this burst of creative activity in the Jewish world. Early formulations of contemporary Jewish meditation have been influenced by Eastern religious traditions being marketed for American consumption. These traditions share little with the theological foundations of Judaism. Critics of Jewish meditation point out that certain fundamental elements of Jewish spirituality are lacking as many Jews pursue meditation. One such element is the notion of "piety."

By "piety," I mean the commitment to a lifestyle that enhances the contemplative life and ensures that meditation is not an isolated component in one's religious quest, but merely a part of a life already permeated with sanctity. The Pious One (a term used in talmudic and medieval literature) is a spiritual model in Judaism that has one goal only: achieving an intimate relationship with the Holy. This, in turn, draws the Holy into the material world.

If we look at the map of Jewish contemplative circles in Jewish history, certain characteristics are almost always present. In the past, Jewish contemplative life (like that of Christianity, Islam, Buddhism, and Hinduism) was almost always an elitist enterprise that demanded asceticism of the group that practiced meditation and a deep commitment to communal life. Contemplative life in Judaism never abandoned *mitzvot* ("commandments," good deeds) as the primary vehicle for the mystical and contemplative experience. The triad of faith, piety, and ritual has almost always served as the fulcrum of the Jewish contemplative life. If faith in God and Torah is the internal core of Jewish spirituality, then piety is its orientation and ritual its externalization. To abandon this model for a simpler model of contemplation does injustice to the history and practice of Jewish contemplation.

HALACHAH AS ART

Many of today's traditionally minded Jews are enamored with how well technology lends itself to the exactness of halachic practice and seems to make contemporary rituals far more "halachically" legitimate (at least in the external sense) than was that of our pretechnological predecessors. One can argue that this has always been the case, that technology should be integrated into halachic discourse because this would let the halachic community more scrupulously observe the commandments. The danger in this approach emerges when science and technology move from the periphery to the center of the halachic process. The broad halachic foundations of Judaism cannot be based in the realm of the practical. As Jews, we are perennially challenged by Paul's critique of Judaism as "Law contra Spirit." We must meet that challenge by the constant renewal of Spirit within Jewish life. Paul's criticism is not foreign to Judaism. Its roots lie in the prophetic critique of Jewish practice that has lost its pietistic core. When Isaiah warned against "performing the *mitzvot* by rote," he was saying that any religion based merely upon ritual observance is flawed. Meditation as a broad halachic foundation for the pietistic nature of Jewish ritual life can be one contemporary response to the dangers of *mitzvot* becoming hollow and mechanical. Yet, meditation must reformulate and breathe new life into the ritualistic life and not present itself as an alternative; otherwise, great violence is done to the tradition.

One model to reformulate and renew *halachah* is "*halachah* as art*.*" By this, I mean that *halachah* should facilitate the expression of the creative impulse of the Jewish will.

Jewish meditation must utilize this transformative model precisely because the Jewish mystical tradition is transformative. The world is never abandoned; it is sanctified. This is key. *Halachah* is never abandoned; it is "artist-ized." Just as artists submit to the creative power within themselves, truly pious persons submit to ritual because it gives form to the Divine in her own being.

Painters, dancers, or musicians submit to two mutually inclusive models of obedience. First, they submit to some *internal* mechanism that enables inspiration to assume form. Second, they submit to an *external* medium that determines what that form will take. The contemplative must submit to the inner nature of their creative instinct, guided by a submission to the "still small voice" of the Divine. Creativity begins with listening.

For the contemplative Jew in the past, *halachah* was a form of yoga, and the halachic life was a devotional "dance" that made concrete one's yearning for closeness to God. The meditative life developed as a further enhancement of that yogic dance in which the practitioner would observe and experience via meditation how each physical act could ascend into the celestial spheres, where it would join the everchanging *sefirotic* (qualities of God made manifest in the world) dance, which channeled the *Shefa* (the Divine ever-flow) as it filtered down into the world. As a famous Hungarian Hasidic master from the late eighteenth century wrote:

...the essential message of the...*Sh'ma* [is] to unify all of the worlds and all of the souls that exist in the Collective Soul of Israel and raise them up to the Infinite Source *(Ein Sof)*. All of this is done with Ultimate Concern *(Mesirat Nefesh)* for God. Only then His Essential Infinite Light is drawn into the world. We [have the capacity] to raise the worlds up to their Primordial Root, to No-thingness *(Ayin)* through the medium of Torah and Mitzvot. Subsequently His...life-force gives renewed life to the worlds. If one would ask, "What is this devotion to us...?", the answer would be this [devotion] is...[His Will]...that [the world should be maintained] via an arousal from below by means of Torah and Mitzvot....[1]

Jewish meditation does not share the passive nature of certain Eastern practices. It never disempowers human action, nor does it demand total submission. Its goal is never pure transcendence. Even the submission to God as the No-thing *(ayin)* demands continuous human participation. The transformation of *halachah* from mere technology to art is accomplished when our concrete acts are seen as an ongoing spiritual practice rather than simple obedience. Meditation as the impetus for external practice is the soul of the contemplative Jewish life.

But how can we "moderns" return to piety? This is the most arduous challenge we face as modern Jews in search of the contemplative life.

THE ANTI-MODERNISM OF PIETY— "STEPPING OUT" INTO SINCERITY

Piety and faith run against the grain of many of our modern sensibilities. Piety is not an easy path for any contemporary society, since piety demands deep sincerity and humility. We are reared in a world where cynicism and irony are the foundations for the way we see the world. We are trapped in attempting to renew the meditative life because we are unconsciously rooted in the very social and technological foundations we cry out against. We need to reformulate terms to meet our unique situation. We need to "step out" into the desert long enough to see the cynicism in ourselves. Indeed, the Greek word for "ecstasy" (*ex-tasis*) means "stepping out." Traditional society encouraged sincerity, which provided aspiring mystics with a foundation from which they could "step out" of the finite self and enter into the realm of the Divine. This notion poses a problem for moderns because we are often not reared with sincerity as a high-ranking value.

Modern practitioners of the contemplative life must begin their journey with a step that may have been unnecessary for our premodern counterparts. We must begin with a modern "stepping out," a pre-ecstatic exercise that makes ecstasy possible. We need to "step out" of the fact that we are always outside ourselves. We need to step out of the modern pursuit of objectivity and *into* the calculated pursuit of sincerity. A first step to do this is to acknowledge our cynicism and consciously "step out" of it.

MEDITATIVE MODELS FOR SINCERITY

Prayer and meditation transform the mundane into the holy by gathering the "mundaneness" of everyday life (including our cynicism) and "stepping out" of its illusory self.

This idea is exemplified in the following paraphrase of a Hasidic custom of turning to the door during the last chorus of the *Lecha Dodi* prayer, which is the climax of the *Kabbalat Shabbat* (Welcoming the Sabbath) liturgy formulated in sixteenth-century Safed. Rabbi Zaddok Kohen Rabinowitz of Lublin, who died in 1900, suggested that the custom of "turning" represents the physical recognition that this moment is the culmination of the recitation of the psalms that make up the body of the *Kabbalat Shabbat* liturgy. Each psalm is intended to fix a particular day of the week and repair it from whatever evils have occurred during it. Yet after concluding the sixth psalm, says Rabbi Zaddok, we realize that we still have not gathered all the mundaneness of the week that needs sanctification. Therefore, he says, we "turn" back to the mundane world even as we travel to the sacred space of Shabbat. In our turning, we are saying to God, "Master of the World, I have tried to gather all that I have not sanctified all week. Yet, something is left behind because I was not sincere enough in my devotion. I was not able to be in the moment to complete the act with sincerity and simplicity. In my deficient cynical posture I may have fulfilled God's will, but I left the world behind. I therefore turn back to that which remains, and I simultaneously turn to You. Let sincerity allow me to finally 'step out' of my inability to be inside enough to gather my belongings so I can responsibly 'step in' to Shabbat." In this light, Shabbat becomes the "overcoming" of modernity.

THE IDOLATRY OF COMPARTMENTALIZING OUR LIVES

The difficulty of creating a viable modern spiritual personality is partially the result of compartmentalizing our lives. But the reformulation of Judaism demands two interrelated components. The first is a theory of an Absolute, whether this be God, the

Collective Unconscious, or some other image.

The second is a notion of relation and *relationship*. Martin Buber writes about this when he says that Judaism must contain a notion of the Absolute that is "other" and the devotional act of worship must take place through the relational act. Not relation to the self, but relation as an act by which we can make the finite other into an Absolute Other. In this way, "faith" can be maintained.

The human being as *tzelim Elohim*, the image of God in the world, bears the responsibility of sanctifying the mundane. First, we must sanctify the self to reactivate the dysfunction of the Divine image through decompartmentalizing our own psyches. In this realm, meditation can have a crucial role in the contemporary plight of the religious seeker. Such a procedure of healthy renewal requires a context, a frame, and a model. The context is *mitzvot,* the frame is piety, and the model is the *tzaddik,* the Pious One. Together, these will carry the redemptive message of ancient Israel.

✳

It is appropriate that the last teaching should be **Nan Fink**'s. Her insight into practice resonates with hope and optimism. Modest concerning her own accomplishments as a meditation teacher, she exemplifies the role of the teacher as someone who points in the direction of the possibility inherent in contemplative practice —regardless of whether the practitioner is ultra-Orthodox or untouched by ritual.

---

22 Notes from a Beginning Meditation Teacher

NAN FINK

When I converted to Judaism in the mid-1980s, I never thought I would teach Jewish meditation. I was drawn to the prayers in Jewish services and especially to the quiet moments in the *Amidah*. But I knew nothing about Jewish meditation.

But then, who did? At that time, Jewish meditation was barely discussed. Like a lot of Jews, I thought that meditation was an esoteric part of Eastern religions or that its sole purpose was to help one relax. It seemed disloyal to me, the new convert, to even consider exploring meditation.

Still, I felt a yearning for stillness. During the Shabbat morning service, I was aware of descending into a meditative state. All the words blurred together as I went beyond myself into a realm that seemed holy. And the singing—it, too, transported me.

But what about other times, especially when I was alone? I assumed that if the tradition says there must be a minyan to begin prayer, then the presence of community is required for meditation. I didn't yet understand that Jewish tradition sanctions Jews to meditate by themselves.

I began to meditate alone, however, as part of my morning *davvening* (prayer). Instead of saying all the prayers, I focused on the deeper meaning of each part of the *Shacharit* (morning) service, beginning with *"Modeh Ani,"* the morning prayer of thanksgiving. I'd sit in front of my bedroom window, first looking out at the bamboo and the olive tree, then closing my eyes. In that quiet, I focused on gratitude to God for my body and for returning my soul to my physical self after the previous night's sleep. When my mind wandered, as it inevitably did, I'd gently bring it back to the task at hand.

This was the morning service's beginning meditation. Through it, and the ones that followed, I learned to focus my thoughts. Each day was different, depending on my mood and my general state of being. Sometimes my mind darted from concern to concern, and I was hardly able to stay with the image. But often I could sustain this long enough to experience a wondrous sensation of closeness with the Divine, and I was filled with joy.

Eventually, meditation became central to my spiritual life. The meditative state was now so familiar that I could enter it at other times of the day. I wrapped myself in the melody of a *niggun*, a wordless melody, on the way to work. A late afternoon meditation refreshed me so much that I could return to my computer with greater clarity. At night, I used the words of the *Sh'ma* as the guiding image of my meditation.

THE CLARITY OF BEING GROUNDED

Meditation became a way of life, rather than a few minutes' feel-good "hit." I soon noticed its results: I became a clearer person; I observed the inevitable wanderings of my mind; I saw what was "on my mind" and realized that I was far more than the workings of my own mind. As I experienced myself in relationship to the Divine through meditation, I was less at the mercy of my thoughts. I had the ability to enter that state of being that is beyond thinking, that state called *devekut* in Jewish mysticism.

All my life, I've sometimes felt adrift amid others' demands and desires. I might lose track of myself and become scattered. When my meditation is strong, however, I become more grounded. I know who I am, and I know what I think.

As I have become more self-defined through meditation, I have also opened up to the presence of the Divine. These moments of connection seem infinite, although they soon pass. Yet, their effect lingers, and I increasingly feel the presence of God, even when I am not meditating. I experience that I am not alone, and I am supported, guided, and accompanied by the Divine as I move through my day. I now teach Jewish meditation. Because my Hebrew skills are limited, I look to others to uncover and illuminate the practices from the kabbalistic tradition. But I can help others understand meditation as I've experienced it in my own life.

In my classes, I've noticed that each person responds differently to meditation. Some love the *niggun* that I use to begin a meditation session; they could sing it for hours, finding the connection with the Divine that I consider to be the point of meditation. Others can barely make it through five minutes of chanting.

Most people are drawn to silence. In meditation sessions, I always give my students an image or a word on which to focus. They may change something in my instructions to make it better for themselves. Afterward, they like to talk about the experience.

WHO IS READY TO MEDITATE?

I haven't yet met a person who is not suited for meditation. The kabbalistic description of the perfect meditator as "forty, married, and male" certainly doesn't seem to hold, although the meditation sessions at Chochmat HaLev in Berkeley attract a fair share of students who are in their forties. No longer believing that they can control their destiny, they hunger for spiritual experience. Yet some of my most interested students are in their twenties, so I hesitate to draw any conclusions about who is ready to meditate.

My students speak of their resistance to meditation: They're too busy. It takes too much time. They can't do it right. And what does it accomplish, anyhow?

Underneath all this, I hear their fear. Perhaps they will discover a painful truth about themselves. Perhaps they'll fall off the edge of an emotional precipice. Maybe the Divine presence will turn out to be a terrible nightmare. Even worse, maybe it will be absolutely unreachable.

Many students have never been alone in silence before. They've always surrounded themselves with people and activity, a defense against the unknown. With them, I proceed slowly, respecting their fears. One rabbi I know always keeps his eyes open when leading a meditation session so his students can find safety in eye contact with him. I love the gentle caring of this

man. Sometimes I, too, provide this for my students if I sense
they need it.

I understand their fear because I remember how frightening meditation was for me at first. Several decades ago, when I
first heard about meditation, I tried it. This was a mantra meditation, the only kind that I knew existed. But I had too many
emotional demons at the time, and my mind wandered to scary
places. If I had had a good teacher, I might have stayed with it.
Instead, I became cynical and laughed at those who "stared at
their bellybuttons." It took becoming a Jew for me to discover
through *davvening* the power of meditation.

RECLAIMING OUR PAST, OPENING UP THE FUTURE

Jews from all parts of the Jewish world attend our meditation
sessions. Those who are religious seek to deepen their practice;
secular Jews yearn to find a way to connect to the tradition of
their birth. They sense that here, finally, is a possibility they can
embrace. Jews and non-Jews who have had other spiritual practices come to us, hoping to find something even more meaningful.
To them, Jewish meditation is less suspect than Jewish prayer
or a life of *mitzvot*. Always they are surprised. "Jewish meditation? We didn't know it exists."

Jewish meditation is not an end in itself, although it can
be an extremely powerful experience. To me, it is one part of a
Jewish spiritual practice. For many students, it is their first connection—or reconnection—with Judaism. As they learn to
meditate, they become interested in other aspects of Jewish spiritual practice, such as observing Shabbat, studying Torah, or
learning prayers. They enlarge their practice to include these,

although for some, meditation will always be at the core of their spiritual discipline.

Most students are interested in a Judaism that is egalitarian and nonpatriarchal. Also committed to this, I'm careful about the images and words upon which I meditate. I am not compelled to incorporate everything from past centuries, and I attempt to use practices that are congruent with late twentieth-century consciousness.

I notice that more men than women lead Jewish meditation. Perhaps men can more readily assume the authority of such a position. Or perhaps women are slow to respond to the opportunity. But I am concerned that women's sensibility be as much a part of contemporary Jewish meditative practice as men's. This is our opportunity to reclaim those parts of the past that correspond to our current understanding of gender.

I envisage an age in which Jewish meditation opens the gates of spiritual understanding for huge numbers of Jews. Aryeh Kaplan writes about a time in Israel at the end of the biblical period when more than one million Israelites meditated regularly. The image fills me with delight and excitement. If they were doing that then, think what we can do now.

✳

Best Practices

Best Practices: A Distillation of Techniques and Outlook

AVRAM DAVIS

This book is full of many wonderfully cogent and wise ideas and techniques to help us begin to meditate and to orient us along the path of meditation. From these, I have extracted the following list that essentially divides a successful meditation discipline into two key components. The first is developing the right attitude; the second is using the right techniques, especially those that are appropriate for your present state of discipline and practice and your readiness to experience different realms of consciousness. Knowing which techniques to use is most important if you are a relative newcomer to meditation.

Attitude means the way in which we frame our questions and how we answer them or seek answers to them. Without a proper attitude, no technique, no matter how valuable or potent, will have long-lasting worth. And since every technique is essentially anchored in attitude (hopefully a proper one), for that attitude to be strengthened and perpetuated, it must be linked to a strong technique that we practice again and again.

ATTITUDE: OPENNESS, DILIGENCE, HUMOR

✳ One basic question that helps shape proper attitude is the question of self. When we ask ourselves major questions of life, we should ask, Who's talking and who's listening?

As Lawrence Kushner points out in his teaching, "Silencing the Inner Voice(s)," "The fact that we can hold these interior conversations with our 'selves' means that we are fragmented, alienated, broken. If we were whole, then there could be no conversation because there would be no one else in there to talk to....Menachem Mendl of Kotzk, a nineteenth-century Hasidic teacher deliberately misreads Deuteronomy 5:5,...'I stood between God and you.' Menachem Mendl teaches that it is your I, 'your ego that stands between you and God.'"

Since ego is what separates us from God, we must lose ego if we are to make progress in meditation and a spiritual life.

✳ Divinity can be found in this world, and the mundane can be found in Divinity. Rabbi Rami M. Shapiro, in "The Teaching and Practice of Reb Yerachmiel ben Yisrael," points out that ultimately these two worlds are one, though they often do not appear to be so. Reality is sometimes perceived as being "out there" and other times as "in here." Both are valid. They are simply aspects of the same ultimate reality, and both point to ultimate meaning.

✳ Trust yourself. The understanding and wisdom brought about by meditation is useful only to the degree that you experience it. It says in the Psalms, "Taste and know that it is good." That is, experience the benefits of meditation yourself before believing anything. Rabbi David Cooper forcefully makes this point in his teaching, "The Promise of Jewish Meditation." He writes, "Religious traditions are not built on *intellectual* revelation. They're built on something that happens in the *kishkes* (gut)....any faith—Judaism or Islam or Buddhism— is based on a personal revelation that profoundly changed someone's life." Trust yourself and your experience. Everything else will follow from this.

✳ Many of the teachers in this book view Jewish law not as a straitjacket but as a liberating force. One way to think of the law is like art. Shaul Magid, in "Piety Before Ecstasy," writes, "One model to reformulate and renew *halachah* is 'halachah as art.'...*halachah* should facilitate the expression of the creative impulse of the Jewish will." Jewish law is not the enemy. Let it become an extension of your will, nothing more. It will serve you well.

✳ God is *ayin*, nothingness. Nothingness is God. Soul is God, a synonym for nothingness. In his teaching "Why Meditate?" Daniel C. Matt helps us incorporate in our practice the concept that God is nothingness, which is ultimately a synonym for soul. By bringing the mind to a realization of *ayin*, nothingness, we perceive our true self. This true self is the ground of being. It is ultimate reality. Realizing this is essential. First, we realize this in our mind. Then we realize this in our practice. Eventually, the knowledge becomes part of our soul.

✳ There is a need in meditation, and indeed in one's daily practice, to surrender and let go. There is no way around this. While it is true that we are pressured by the imperative nature of our busy lives, meditation practice insists on a discipline of surrender. In "Meditating as a Practicing Jew," Rabbi Sheila Peltz Weinberg points this out very forcefully: "Meditation is...about letting go: letting go of preconceived ideas and gently bringing oneself into the presence of what is, not what we imagine or remember or desire." This teaching is both an attitude and a technique, for it presumes a constant effort of surrender.

✳ The ultimate reality is intimate and personal. It is not distant, removed, or mechanical. Many of the teachers in this collection reiterate this point. Andrea Cohen-Kiener, in "Go to Your Self," emphasizes that the universe is found within our own, personal body, only writ small. As she writes, "Meditation can help us get a handle...from which to watch ourselves so we can be more aware about how we react to things." This attitude of self-awareness is an inherent part of the universe. The more we cultivate it within ourselves, the stronger our practice becomes.

✳ We are what we practice. If we become angry a lot, then essentially we are practicing anger. And we become quite good at it. Conversely, if we practice being joyful, then a joyful person is what we become. We are what we practice. Each of us consciously must decide who and what we want to be— or the circumstances of our life will choose for us.

One way to make such a choice is to calmly be aware of life's situations. By doing this, we begin to clearly see that both pain and joy are inevitable and time limited. We discover that struggling with what is beyond our control causes suffering. We also discover that kind, considered, compassionate response makes life manageable.

✳ The essence of God's reality is joy and blessing. Rabbi Shohama Wiener, along with several of the other teachers, stresses this teaching. While some spiritual paths say that the world is suffering, this is not the perspective of the Jewish path. It is true that there *is* suffering in the world, but the beauty and joy of God are the more fundamental reality. This is not to discount the pain, but underneath even this is joy.

* Rabbi Rami M. Shapiro teaches in "The Teaching and Practice of Reb Yerachmiel ben Yisrael" that the Infinite is already here. God is outside so that we can draw the Divine inside. God is inside so that we can let the Divine merge with the outside.

* Don't be pretentious. Meditation is not brain surgery. In "Notes from a Beginning Meditation Teacher," Nan Fink gives us permission to experiment with our practice—to take it on a bit at a time or to completely immerse ourselves in it, but to guard against too much self-aggrandizement. The practice is, after all, only to benefit us. The speed by which this occurs is completely up to us.

* Wherever you are, that's where you need to start. As I point out in "Jewish Meditation Today and Its Obstacles," it is important not to get hung up on definitions. Many things are "meditation." Many things help us in the transformation that we need to accomplish. At the same time, give yourself time and space to sit and delve inwardly.

* Be diligent. Practice with humor. Much of the Torah deals with life situations. Many of these are amusing, at least in retrospect. Try to keep this humor close to hand. But, also practice your meditation with great resolve.

✳ Meditation does not negate the cognitive. In their teachings, both Susie Schneider and Rabbi Laibl Wolf strive to make this point. The mind informs us and helps direct our actions. But our intellects are not the end-all.

✳ Problems arise when we seriously engage in a spiritual practice like meditation. There may be such obstacles as feeling a loss of meaning or wondering why you are even bothering to meditate. Rabbi Jonathan Omer-Man points out that this is inevitable and that the difficulties are part of the work. The obstacles themselves, as Omer-Man says in "Noble Boredom," can become "points of transformation." But patience is the quality we must cultivate. Patience with your obsessions, with your foolishness, with your difficulties. Patience to keep on with the work.

✳ This whole meditation business is really very communal. Rabbi Alan Lew, in "It Doesn't Matter What You Call It," rightly points out that too much solitary meditation opens us to delusions of Self. We can get overly caught up in our own ego machinations. In a group, we are part of a collective, self-monitoring system, and our mistakes will be fewer, our insights deeper.

✳ Rabbi Lew believes meditation to be, in its deepest sense, a "leave-taking." Feel free to gain insight from meditation, and try to incorporate this insight into your day-to-day living.

✳ Rabbi Rami M. Shapiro teaches meditation is part and parcel of everyday life. "Doing everyday things with a clear and attentive mind awakens us to the fact that we are both apart from and a part of everything else. We discover that from the perspective of *yesh*, we are unique, irreducible, irreplaceable manifestations of God. We discover from the perspective of *ayin* that we are totally interconnected with and dependent upon all other manifestations of God. We are awake to our being and our emptiness simultaneously. And from this we awake to God, the Source and Substance of both."

TECHNIQUE: DISCIPLINE, STUDY, TRADITION

✴ Time is a key factor in developing, keeping, and strengthening your spiritual path, as Rabbi David Zeller stresses in his teaching "A Splendid Way to Live." Shabbat, which is a one-day-a-week withdrawal from technology and work, is a very important time to cultivate one's practice in terms of sitting meditation. It is a time to cultivate *midot*, or personal qualities.

All the teachers in this book believe in the need to observe Shabbat gradually, but steadily. Shabbat is all about time, and all meditation, all spiritual practice, and all spiritual improvement ultimately involve time.

✴ In quiet meditation, let your consciousness ascend into the all-pervading light of the Divine. In his teaching "The Hierarchy of Jewish Meditation," Rabbi Alan Brill directs us to bring this infinite light down, letting it grow and give energy, letting it fill our minds and bodies and wherever we may be. Channel this slowly to avoid being overwhelmed. The purpose of this meditation is to unify the Divine and the mundane.

✴ The use of specific sounds contributes to advancement of our practice. Repetition of these holy words and sounds is a strong technique. In "Opening the Inner Gates," Dr. Edward Hoffman recommends using the commonly known word *shalom*, which means "peace" or "wholeness." As Hoffman writes, "Begin by saying *'shalom'* aloud a few times, gradually elongating its syllables. Now, find a rhythm that feels comfortable, yet empowering, by adjusting the length of the 'shhhhaaa,' 'lo,' and 'mmmmmm' sounds to your preference. They do not have to be of equal length; each can have varying durations." At the end of this exercise, record your thoughts in a journal. While doing this technique, hold on to a feeling of reverence "for the holiness of our inner world."

✳ Chanting works. Rabbi Shefa Gold, in her teaching "That This Song May Be a Witness," introduces us to the ecstatic power of chant. Chant has a unique power to open the heart. As Gold writes, "Repetition [of a chant] became a way to still the mind and open the heart so widely that it felt as if the sacred phrases were planting seeds there."

✳ Rabbi Rami M. Shapiro offers a ten-point outline of practice: meditation, recitation of a sacred phrase, study, focused attention, daily self-assessment of behavior, generosity, random acts of loving-kindness, dream study, ethical consumption of food and other products, and finally, Shabbat.

✳ A straightforward beginning way to meditate is given by Mindy Ribner in "Keeping God Before Me Always." She suggests that you first sit quietly, regulate your breath, and calm your mind. Tell yourself that this meditation is meant to unite the *yod heh* with *vav heh*, the Divine letters of God's

Name. Let yourself picture the connection you are making with all the generations of 5,000 years of Jewish people. All these holy teachers are helping you link together the disparate aspects of God. A beautiful variation on this meditation is to begin with the same relaxing preamble, then open your heart and let the presence of the Divine dwell there. Let yourself feel this presence. Reflect on whether what you want in your life is the same as what God wants for you. From this meditation will arise insights on how to bring God more into your daily life.

As you sit, thought fragments of the day and emotions will begin to surface in your mind. Perceive each of these clearly, and embrace it with affection, for the mind is not your enemy. Then, let the thought fragment go. In the moment that follows the letting go, there will be an opening and a deepening of consciousness. Dov Baer of Mezritch called this "in-between." It is the doorway to *ayin*, to nothingness. As we deepen this in-between space, true wisdom arises. This wisdom we may call "soul." In her teaching "On Mindfulness," Sylvia Boorstein calls this the place of mindfulness. It is a powerful place. Its cultivation is invaluable for a strong meditation practice.

✳ Rabbi Alan Lew embraces the insight of direct seeing. For a moment during the day, try to see whatever it is you are dealing with without barrier or illusion. By doing this, "suddenly the street is beautiful and the quality of light is extraordinary...." This is the practice of insightful seeing.

✳ Rabbi David Zeller in his teaching "A Splendid Way to Live," urges us to see the Divine in the everyday. This is an essential component of meditation: the everydayness of perspective. Each of our emotional traits needs to become "a channel for the highest aspect of that trait—its Godly aspect...." This perspective is not a detachment from the world, but a passionate attachment to all the beauties put on the earth.

* A key teaching from Rabbi Shohama Wiener is to bless what you eat, bless what you drink, bless what you wear, bless your relationships with other people and with nature. Make many blessings every day, Wiener advises in "Healing and Meditation." Jewish tradition says we should make one hundred blessings a day. Saying blessings unites the spiritual and the mundane.

* Tell stories. This deceptively simple recommendation from Rabbi Lynn Gottlieb in "Meditation and Women's Kabbalah" is a striking bit of advice. It is simple but goes straight to the root of practice. As Gottlieb says, "Telling a story can be compared to building a home or sacred lodge for the imagination. This lodge is a place of giving witness to one's truth, of opening one's voice and body, of surrendering to the story's own transcendent wisdom." Learn the stories of the tradition, and tell them with your own words. Make them your own, and through them your own stories will become avenues of understanding.

* Words have power. Just as there are power "spots" on the planet, so are there power objects or especially powerful images. Words have great power and so do their building blocks, the letters. The Hebrew letters are a powerful lens of meditation. We can use them, each individual, as a meditation

object to strengthen our concentration and deepen our insight, for each letter has a resonance unique to it. The tradition considers the letters to be the building blocks of the universe. Rabbi Steve Fisdel is acutely aware of this in his teaching, "Meditation as Our Own Jacob's Ladder." He writes, "The Kabbalists...taught that each of the twenty-two letters of the Hebrew alphabet represents a primal cosmic force that is a fundamental building block of Creation. Each letter is a different light, a different energy. The combination of any group of letters is understood to be an interaction of primal energies, the result of which is the emergence of some specific reality within the universe." Under the tutelage of a trained teacher, use the letters as meditation foci.

✳ Edward Hoffman and other teachers recommend this beginning meditation: First, relax and let your mind's eye perceive a point of light. Inhale slowly, and draw this light into your body. Feel it circulate through all of your limbs; feel it vitalizing your spirit and emotions. The light will begin to increase in clarity. Inside of your body, let it travel where it will, especially allowing it to fill the places that need healing.

Exhale, and sense the light leaving through your feet. As it leaves, it removes any tensions and negativities that you may have been harboring, either consciously or unconsciously. Feel yourself becoming refreshed and cleansed.

Breathe a few more times. With each breath, feel connected to God.

✳ Meditation does not necessarily mean sitting still. You can meditate standing, walking, dancing, or lying down. It can be done through emotions, thinking, learning, and contemplating and through art, music, or song. The variety of practice exists so everyone can find their own way (or ways) to transform themselves and the world.

✳ Studying holy texts lets your mind directly access that intense revelation of light and consciousness that happened at Sinai. Study hard, but deeply. The point of study is not memorization or clever argumentation but to bring you closer to the Divine.

✳ Sing. Eat. Love. Embrace. Laugh. Cry. Give. Surrender. Sit and contemplate Self. You will find that you will finally be drawn into the silence, a silence that is always singing.

Notes

Introduction: The Heart of Meditation

1. Moses Cordovero, *Introduction to Kabbalah: An Annotated Translation of His Or Ne'erav*, trans. Ira Robinson (New York: Yeshiva University Press, 1994), p. 89.

2. Issachar Baer of Zlotshov, in Daniel C. Matt, *The Essential Kabbalah* (San Francisco: HarperSanFrancisco, 1995), p. 72.

3. Azriel of Gerona, in Daniel C. Matt, *The Essential Kabbalah* (San Francisco: HarperSanFrancisco, 1995), p. 117.

Silencing the Inner Voice(s)

Much of this teaching was originally delivered as a sermon at the Hebrew Union College–Jewish Institute of Religion, New York City, October 12, 1989 and appeared in different form in my book *God Was in This Place and I, i Did Not Know* (Woodstock, Vt.: Jewish Lights Publishing, 1991).

1. Mordechai HaKohen, *Al HaTorah* (Jerusalem, 1968), pp. 489–90; cf. also *Sefer Hasidim*, cited in *Itturay Torah*, vol. VI, p. 43; similarly, Rabbi Dov Baer of Mezritch, *Mamre Hasidim* in *Itturay Torah*, vol. II, p. 257. Cf. also "...To kill off selfhood, for 'Torah does not exist'—is not really alive and one with the source—except in the one who kills himself..." and Green's comment, "A counsel of ascetic devotion to a life of study has here been reread as a mystical counsel on the need for ego death in the one who has discovered God within his own self." Menahem Nahum of Chernobyl, *Upright Practices, the Light of the Eyes,* trans. Arthur Green (New York: Paulist Press, 1982), p. 186.

2. Rabbi Hayyim of Krosno, in Martin Buber, *Tales of the Hasidim: The Early Masters* (New York: Schocken, 1947), p. 174.

3. Moshe Idel, *Kabbalah: New Perspectives* (New Haven: Yale University Press, 1988), p. 35.

4. Cf. Moshe Idel, *Studies in Ecstatic Kabbalah* (Albany: State University of New York Press, 1988), pp. 11–12. Because of this correlation, it seems that the phrase, "I-I" is an exclamation by a mystic, indicating his awareness of becoming divine.

5. *Or Ha-Me'ir*, trans. Daniel C. Matt, p. 95; cf. also Buber translation in Martin Buber, *Tales of the Hasidim: The Early Masters* (New York: Schocken, 1947), p. 174.

6. Martin Buber, *Hasidism and Modern Man,* p. 195.

7. Cf. "the worshiper continues to recite the words of prayer, but it is no longer the worshiper who speaks them. Rather it is the Presence who speaks through him. In that prayerful return to the source one has reached the highest human state, becoming nought but the passive instrument for the ever self-proclaiming praise of God." Arthur Green and Barry W. Holtz, ed. and trans., *Your Word is Fire: The Hasidic Masters on Contemplative Prayer* (Woodstock, Vt.: Jewish Lights Publishing, 1993), p. 14.

8. Idel, *Kabbalah: New Perspectives*, pp. 39 ff.

9. Idel, *Studies in Ecstatic Kabbalah*, p. 46.

10. E.g., *Berakhot* 6a: Rabbi Nahman ben Isaac asks Rabbi Hiyya ben Abin, "What is written in God's *Tefillin*?" 'Who is like your people Israel, one nation on the earth'...The Holy One said to Israel: You have made Me a unique entity in the world [by reciting the *Sh'ma*]...and I shall make you a unique entity in the world, [with the words in My *Tefillin*]." Cf. also *Itturay Torah*, vol. I, p. 126, "in the name of R. Meir of Premishlan."

11. Menachem Nahum of Chernobyl, *Upright Practices, the Light of the Eyes,* p. 136.

12. Idel, *Kabbalah: New Perspectives*, p. 44.

13. *Likkutei Moharan* 21:11; cf. also "There is nothing besides the presence of God; being itself is derived from God and the presence of the Creator remains in each created thing." Menahem Nahum of Chernobyl, *Upright Practices, the Light of the Eyes*, p. 100.

Jewish Meditation Today and Its Obstacles

1. Gershom Scholem, *Kabbalah* (New York: Meridian: New American Library, 1974), p. 369.

2. Ibid. p. 174.

3. Bachya Ben Asher, *Kad HaKemach: Encyclopedia of Torah Thoughts*, trans. and ed. Charles Chavel (New York: Shilo Publishing, 1980), p. 30.

4. Ecclesiastes *Rabbah*, in *Sefer Aggada: The Book of Legends*, ed. H. Bialik and Y. Ravnitzky (New York: Schocken, 1992), p. 677.

Piety Before Ecstasy

1. R. Zvi Hirsch Eichenstein of Zhidacov, *Sur me Ra V Aseh Tov* (Pest, 1942), p. 131. Cf. I.L. Jacobs, *Turn Aside from Evil and Do Good* (London, 1995).

Glossary

Adonai—One of the names of God.

Alef—First letter of the Hebrew alphabet. Also numerically stands for "one," which, in turn, represents the One, God, unity, etc.

Chesed—Loving-kindness; joyful compassion.

Chevre—The community of spiritual practitioners.

Davven—Prayer, usually communal.

Devekut—Rapturous attachment. One of the four states of mind cultivated in Jewish meditation practice.

Ein Sof—Literally, "without end." One of the names of God. It is the idea of God as process, rather than as object.

Gan Eden—The Garden of Eden.

Gemilut chesed—The practice of *chesed*.

Gilgul Hanefesh—Reincarnation.

Halachah—Literally meaning "the way," it is generally used to refer to Jewish religious law.

Hashgachah Pratit—Divine providence.

Hitbodedut—Usually defined as inner-directed meditation.

Hitbonenut—Usually defined as outer-directed meditation.

Kavvanah—Focused, or passionate intentionality.

Kavvanot—Recitations or directed thought constructions used in meditation or worship.

Ma'ariv—Evening prayer service.

Maaseh Bereshith—Acts of creation.

Maaseh HaMerkavah—Acts of the chariot-type of ascension used in meditation.

Mashpiah—Spiritual director.

Mehitzah—Ritual wall separating the genders in orthodox synagogues.

Mezuzah—Box on the doorpost of Jewish homes, containing the *Sh'ma* prayer.

Minchah—Afternoon prayer service.

Midrash—Rabbinic genre of lore often based on biblical texts; legend in the rabbinic style.

Mishnah Brura—A book of Jewish law.

Mishneh Torah—Twelfth-century law code written by Maimonides.

Mochin gadlut—Great mind; enlightenment.

Modeh Ani—A morning prayer of gratitude.

Musar—A guide and practice to moral life. Seen as indispensable for a deep and sustained meditation practice.

Nefesh—The animal soul. The simplest soul humans have.

Neshamah—A higher soul humans possess.

Niggun—A wordless melody.

Olam Hasheker—The world of lies, usually used pejoratively about this world.

Onesh—Punishment.

Perush—Explanation.

Ratzon—Will.

Ruach—Spirit, wind, essence.

Tefillah—Prayer and/or meditation.

Teshuvah—"Repentance"; "return." Used to refer to transformation through recognition of the past's incorrect behavior and willingness to change and transform.

Yechidah—Unity; private meeting with a teacher.

Yeshiva bocher—A seminary student.

Yetzer Harah—The negative impulse or energy.

Yetzer Hatov—The positive impulse or energy.

Yetziat Mitzraim—The going out from Egypt.

Zohar—A book of Jewish mysticism written during medieval times, in the form of a commentary on the Torah.

Suggested Readings and Materials

Boorstein, Sylvia. *Don't Just Do Something, Sit There: A Mindfulness Retreat with Sylvia Boorstein* (San Francisco: HarperSanFrancisco, 1996).

Buxbaum, Yitzhak. *Jewish Spiritual Practices* (Northvale, N.J.: Jason Aronson, 1994).

Cooper, David A. *A Heart of Stillness: A Complete Guide to Learning the Art of Meditation.* (Woodstock, Vt.: SkyLight Paths Publishing, 1999).

Cooper, David A. *Silence, Simplicity and Solitude: A Complete Guide to Spiritual Retreat.* (Woodstock, Vt.: SkyLight Paths Publishing, 1999).

Cordovero, Moses ben Jacob. *The Palm Tree of Deborah.* Trans. Louis Jacobs (New York: Hermon Press, 1974).

Davis, Avram. *The Way of the Flame: A Guide to the Forgotten Mystical Tradition of Jewish Meditation* (Woodstock, Vt.: Jewish Lights Publishing, 1999).

Fine, Lawrence, ed. *Safed Spirituality* (Mahwah, N.J.: Paulist Press, 1984).

Fink, Nan. *Stranger in the Midst: A Memoir of Spiritual Discovery* (New York: Basic Books, 1997).

Fisdel, Steven A. *The Practice of Kabbalah: Meditation in Judaism* (Northvale, N.J.: Jason Aronson, 1996).

Gold, Shefa. Excellent tapes of chanting are available c/o Rose Mountain, P.O. Box 355, Las Vegas, NM 87701.

Gottleib, Lynn. *She Who Dwells Within: A Feminist Vision of a Renewed Judaism* (San Francisco: HarperSanFrancisco, 1995).

Hoffman, Edward. *The Heavenly Ladder: Kabbalistic Techniques for Inner Growth* (Dorset, UK: Prism Press Ltd., 1996).

Kaplan, Aryeh. *Jewish Meditation: A Practical Guide* (New York: Schocken Books, 1995).

Kushner, Lawrence. *God Was in This Place & I, i Did Not Know: Finding Self, Spirituality, and Ultimate Meaning* (Woodstock, Vt.: Jewish Lights, 1993).

Kushner, Lawrence. *Honey from the Rock: An Easy Introduction to Jewish Mysticism* (Woodstock, Vt.: Jewish Lights, 1990).

Labowitz, Shoni. *Miraculous Living: A Guided Journey in Kabbalah through the Ten Gates of the Tree of Life* (New York: Simon & Schuster, 1996).

Matt, Daniel C. *The Essential Kabbalah: The Heart of Jewish Mysticism* (San Francisco: HarperSanFrancisco, 1996).

Matt, Daniel C. *God & the Big Bang: Discovering Harmony Between Science and Spirituality* (Woodstock, Vt.: Jewish Lights, 1996).

Schachter-Shalomi, Zalman, Jonathan Omer-Man, and Shohama Wiener. *Worlds of Jewish Prayer: A Festschrift in Honor of Rabbi Zalman Schachter-Shalomi* (Northvale, N.J.: Jason Aronson, 1994).

Schneider, Susie. Schneider's ongoing series of spiritual monographs called *A Still Small Voice* is excellent and well worth subscribing to. Contact A Still Small Voice: Correspondence Teachings in Classic Jewish Wisdom by mail at P.O. Box 14503, Jerusalem, Israel, 91141.

Shapiro, Rami M. *Wisdom of the Jewish Sages: A Modern Reading of Pirke Avot* (New York: Bell Tower, 1995).

Verman, Mark. *The History and Varieties of Jewish Meditation* (Northvale, N.J.: Jason Aronson, 1996).

Zeller, David. Helpful tapes on meditation are available through the Network of Conscious Judaism, 105 Militia St., Vallejo, CA 94590-3449. Tel. (707) 552 2199.

About the Editor

Avram Davis is the author of *The Way of the Flame: A Guide to the Forgotten Mystical Tradition of Jewish Meditation* (HarperCollins), an introduction to the practice of meditation within Jewish tradition. He is also founder and co-director of Chochmat HaLev, an independent renewal center of Jewish learning, in Berkeley, California, which can be reached by phone at (510) 704-9687.

About JEWISH LIGHTS Publishing

People of all faiths and backgrounds yearn for books that attract, engage, educate and spiritually inspire.

Our principal goal is to stimulate thought and help all people learn about who the Jewish People are, where they come from, and what the future can be made to hold. While people of our diverse Jewish heritage are the primary audience, our books speak to people in the Christian world as well and will broaden their understanding of Judaism and the roots of their own faith.

We bring to you authors who are at the forefront of spiritual thought and experience. While each has something different to say, they all say it in a voice that you can hear.

Our books are designed to welcome you and then to engage, stimulate and inspire. We judge our success not only by whether or not our books are beautiful and commercially successful, but by whether or not they make a difference in your life.

We at Jewish Lights take great care to produce beautiful books that present meaningful spiritual content in a form that reflects the art of making high quality books. Therefore, we want to acknowledge those who contributed to the production of this book.

EDITORIAL & PROOFREADING
Sandra Korinchak / Jennifer Goneau

PRODUCTION
Maria O'Donnell

COVER/TEXT DESIGN
Glenn Suokko

PRINTING AND BINDING
Lake Book, Melrose Park, Illinois

New from Jewish Lights

"WHO IS A JEW?"
Conversations, Not Conclusions
by *Meryl Hyman*

Who is "Jewish enough" to be considered a Jew? And by whom?

Meryl Hyman courageously takes on this timely and controversial question to give readers the perspective necessary to draw their own conclusions. Profound personal questions of identity are explored in conversations with Jew and non-Jew in the U.S., Israel and England.

6" x 9", 272 pp. Quality Paperback, ISBN 1-58023-052-0 **$16.95**
HC, ISBN 1-879045-76-1 **$23.95**

THE JEWISH GARDENING COOKBOOK
Growing Plants and Cooking for Holidays & Festivals
by *Michael Brown*

Wherever you garden—a city apartment windowsill or on an acre—with the fruits and vegetables of your own labors, the traditional repasts of Jewish holidays and celebrations can be understood in many new ways!

Gives easy to follow instructions for raising foods that have been harvested since ancient times. Provides carefully selected, tasty and easy to prepare recipes using these traditional foodstuffs for holidays, festivals, and life cycle events. Clearly illustrated with more than 30 fine botanical illustrations. For beginner and professional alike.

6" x 9", 224 pp. HC, ISBN 1-58023-004-0 **$21.95**

WANDERING STARS
An Anthology of Jewish Fantasy & Science Fiction
Edited by *Jack Dann;* with an Introduction by *Isaac Asimov*

Jewish science fiction and fantasy? *Yes!* Here are the distinguished contributors: Bernard Malamud, Isaac Bashevis Singer, Isaac Asimov, Robert Silverberg, Harlan Ellison, Pamela Sargent, Avram Davidson, Geo. Alec Effinger, Horace L. Gold, Robert Sheckley, William Tenn and Carol Carr. Pure enjoyment. We laughed out loud reading it. A 25th Anniversary Classic Reprint.

6" x 9", 272 pp. Quality Paperback, ISBN 1-58023-005-9 **$16.95**

THE ENNEAGRAM AND KABBALAH
Reading Your Soul
by *Rabbi Howard A. Addison*

What do the Enneagram and *Kabbalah* have in common? Together, can they provide a powerful tool for self-knowledge, critique, and transformation?

How can we distinguish between acquired personality traits and the essential self hidden underneath?

6" x 9", 176 pp. Quality Paperback Original, ISBN 1-58023-001-6 **$15.95**

Or phone, fax or mail to: **JEWISH LIGHTS** Publishing
Sunset Farm Offices, Route 4 • P.O. Box 237 • Woodstock, Vermont 05091
Tel (802) 457-4000   Fax (802) 457-4004   www.jewishlights.com
Credit card orders **(800) 962-4544** (9AM–5PM ET Monday–Friday)
Generous discounts on quantity orders. SATISFACTION GUARANTEED. Prices subject to change.

Spirituality

•AWARD WINNER•

HOW TO BE A PERFECT STRANGER, In 2 Volumes
A Guide to Etiquette in Other People's
Religious Ceremonies
Edited by *Stuart M. Matlins & Arthur J. Magida*

"A book that belongs in every living room,
library and office!"

Explains the rituals and celebrations of America's major religions/denominations, helping an interested guest to feel comfortable, participate to the fullest extent possible, and avoid violating anyone's religious principles. Answers practical questions from the perspective of *any* other faith.

VOL. 1: America's Largest Faiths

VOL. 1 COVERS: Assemblies of God • Baptist • Buddhist • Christian Science • Churches of Christ • Disciples of Christ • Episcopalian • Greek Orthodox • Hindu • Islam • Jehovah's Witnesses • Jewish • Lutheran • Methodist • Mormon • Presbyterian • Quaker • Roman Catholic • Seventh-day Adventist • United Church of Christ

6" x 9", 432 pp. Hardcover, ISBN 1-879045-39-7 **$24.95**

VOL. 2: Other Faiths in America

VOL. 2 COVERS: African American Methodist Churches • Baha'i • Christian and Missionary Alliance • Christian Congregation • Church of the Brethren • Church of the Nazarene • Evangelical Free Church of America • International Church of the Foursquare Gospel • International Pentecostal Holiness Church • Mennonite/Amish • Native American • Orthodox Churches • Pentecostal Church of God • Reformed Church of America • Sikh • Unitarian Universalist • Wesleyan

6" x 9", 416 pp. HC, ISBN 1-879045-63-X **$24.95**

GOD & THE BIG BANG
Discovering Harmony Between Science & Spirituality
by *Daniel C. Matt*

•AWARD WINNER•

Mysticism and science: What do they have in common? How can one enlighten the other? By drawing on modern cosmology and ancient Kabbalah, Matt shows how science and religion can together enrich our spiritual awareness and help us recover a sense of wonder and find our place in the universe.

"This poetic new book...helps us to understand the human meaning of creation."
—*Joel Primack, leading cosmologist, Professor of*
Physics, University of California, Santa Cruz

6" x 9", 216 pp. Quality Paperback, ISBN 1-879045-89-3 **$16.95**; HC, ISBN -48-6 **$21.95**

MINDING THE TEMPLE OF THE SOUL
Balancing Body, Mind, & Spirit through Traditional Jewish
Prayer, Movement, & Meditation
by *Tamar Frankiel* and *Judy Greenfeld*

This new spiritual approach to physical health introduces readers to a spiritual tradition that affirms the body and enables them to reconceive their bodies in a more positive light. Relying on Kabbalistic teachings and other Jewish traditions, it shows us how to be more responsible for our own psychological and physical health. Focuses on the discipline of prayer, simple Tai Chi–like exercises and body positions, and guides the reader throughout, step by step, with diagrams, sketches and meditations.

7"x 10", 184 pp. Quality Paperback Original, illus., ISBN 1-879045-64-8 **$16.95**

Audiotape of the Blessings, Movements & Meditations (60-min. cassette) **$9.95**
Videotape of the Movements & Meditations (46-min. VHS) **$20.00**

Spirituality—The Kushner Series

EYES REMADE FOR WONDER
A Lawrence Kushner Reader
Introduction by *Thomas Moore*

A treasury of insight from one of the most creative spiritual thinkers in America. Whether you are new to Kushner or a devoted fan, this is the place to begin. With samplings from each of Kushner's works, and a generous amount of new material, this is a book to be savored, to be read and reread, each time discovering deeper layers of meaning in our lives. Offers something unique to both the spiritual seeker and the committed person of faith.

6" x 9", 240 pp. Quality PB, ISBN 1-58023-042-3 **$16.95**; HC, ISBN -014-8 **$23.95**

INVISIBLE LINES OF CONNECTION
Sacred Stories of the Ordinary
by *Lawrence Kushner*

Through his everyday encounters with family, friends, colleagues and strangers, Kushner takes us deeply into our lives, finding flashes of spiritual insight in the process.

5½" x 8½", 160 pp. Quality Paperback, ISBN 1-879045-98-2 **$15.95**
HC, ISBN -52-4 **$21.95**

•AWARD WINNER•

HONEY FROM THE ROCK
An Easy Introduction to Jewish Mysticism
by *Lawrence Kushner*

"Quite simply the easiest introduction to Jewish mysticism you can read."

An introduction to the ten gates of Jewish mysticism and how it applies to daily life.

6" x 9", 168 pp. Quality Paperback, ISBN 1-879045-02-8 **$14.95**

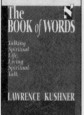

THE BOOK OF WORDS
Talking Spiritual Life, Living Spiritual Talk
by *Lawrence Kushner*

In the incomparable manner of his extraordinary *The Book of Letters*, Kushner now lifts up and shakes the dust off primary religious words we use to describe the spiritual dimension of life. For each word Kushner offers us a startling, moving and insightful explication. He concludes with a short exercise that helps unite the spirit of the word with our actions in the world.

6" x 9", 160 pp. 2-color text, Quality PB, ISBN 1-58023-020-2 **$16.95**; HC, ISBN 1-879045-35-4 **$21.95**

THE BOOK OF LETTERS
A Mystical Hebrew Alphabet
by *Rabbi Lawrence Kushner*

In calligraphy by the author. Folktales about and exploration of the mystical meanings of the Hebrew Alphabet. Draws from ancient Judaic sources, weaving Talmudic commentary, Hasidic folktales, and kabbalistic mysteries around the letters.

• **Popular Hardcover Edition** 6"x 9", 80 pp. HC, two colors, inspiring new Foreword. ISBN 1-879045-00-1 **$24.95**

• **Deluxe Gift Edition** 9"x 12", 80 pp. HC, four-color text, ornamentation, in a beautiful slipcase. **$79.95**

•AWARD WINNER•

• **Collector's Limited Edition** 9"x 12", 80 pp. HC, gold-embossed pages, hand-assembled slipcase. With silkscreened print. **Limited to 500 signed and numbered copies.** ISBN 1-879045-04-4 **$349.00**

Spirituality

GOD WAS IN THIS PLACE & I, i DID NOT KNOW
Finding Self, Spirituality & Ultimate Meaning
by *Lawrence Kushner*

Who am I? Who is God? Kushner creates inspiring interpretations of Jacob's dream in Genesis, opening a window into Jewish spirituality for people of all faiths and backgrounds.

6" x 9", 192 pp. Quality Paperback, ISBN 1-879045-33-8 **$16.95**

THE RIVER OF LIGHT
Spirituality, Judaism, Consciousness
by *Lawrence Kushner*

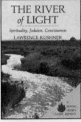

A "manual" for all spiritual travelers who would attempt a spiritual journey in our times. Taking us step by step, Kushner allows us to discover the meaning of our own quest: "to allow the river of light—the deepest currents of consciousness—to rise to the surface and animate our lives."

6" x 9", 180 pp. Quality Paperback, ISBN 1-879045-03-6 **$14.95**

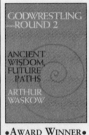

GODWRESTLING—ROUND 2
Ancient Wisdom, Future Paths
by *Arthur Waskow*

This 20th-anniversary sequel to a seminal book of the Jewish renewal movement deals with spirituality in relation to personal growth, marriage, ecology, feminism, politics, and more.

6" x 9", 352 pp. Quality Paperback, ISBN 1-879045-72-9 **$18.95**
HC, ISBN -45-1 **$23.95**

•AWARD WINNER•

ECOLOGY & THE JEWISH SPIRIT
Where Nature & the Sacred Meet
Edited and with Introductions by *Ellen Bernstein*

What is nature's place in our spiritual lives?

A focus on nature is part of the fabric of Jewish thought. Here, experts bring us a richer understanding of the long-neglected themes of nature that are woven through the biblical creation story, ancient texts, traditional law, the holiday cycles, prayer, *mitzvot* (good deeds), and community.

6" x 9", 288 pp. HC, ISBN 1-879045-88-5 **$23.95**

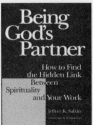

BEING GOD'S PARTNER
How to Find the Hidden Link Between Spirituality and Your Work
by *Jeffrey K. Salkin*; Introduction by *Norman Lear*

Will challenge people of every denomination to reconcile the cares of work and soul. A groundbreaking book about spirituality and the work world, from a Jewish perspective. Offers practical suggestions for balancing your professional life and spiritual self.

6" x 9", 192 pp. Quality Paperback, ISBN 1-879045-65-6 **$16.95**
HC, ISBN -37-0 **$19.95**

Spirituality

SOUL JUDAISM
Dancing with God into a New Era
by *Rabbi Wayne Dosick*

An easy to read introduction to Judaism, and a vision of Judaism's coming new age, *Soul Judaism* can help you add a rich spiritual dimension to your life and help you connect personally and intimately with the divine. A do-it-yourself guide to spirituality, *Soul Judaism* provides simple exercises and suggestions for enriching daily life, drawing upon Jewish meditation, mysticism and the ancient tradition of Kabbalah.

"A very helpful, considerate introductory manual to a richer Jewish life."
—*Rodger Kamenetz, author of* Stalking Elijah

6" x 9", 304 pp. Quality Paperback, ISBN 1-58023-053-9 **$16.95**

GOD WHISPERS
Stories of the Soul, Lessons of the Heart
by *Karyn D. Kedar*

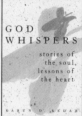

Eloquent stories from the lives of ordinary people teach readers that the joy and pain in our lives have meaning and purpose, and that by fully embracing life's highs and lows, we can enrich our spiritual well-being. Helps us cope with difficulties such as divorce and reconciliation, illness, loss, conflict and forgiveness, loneliness and isolation.

6" x 9", 176 pp. Hardcover, ISBN 1-58023-023-7 **$19.95**

SELF, STRUGGLE & CHANGE
Family Conflict Stories in Genesis
and Their Healing Insights for Our Lives
by *Norman J. Cohen*

How do I find greater wholeness in my life and in my family's life?

Here a modern master of biblical interpretation brings us greater understanding of the ancient text and of ourselves in this intriguing re-telling of conflict between husband and wife, father and son, brothers, and sisters.

6" x 9", 224 pp. Quality Paperback, ISBN 1-879045-66-4 **$16.95**
HC, ISBN -19-2 **$21.95**

VOICES FROM GENESIS
Guiding Us Through the Stages of Life
by *Norman J. Cohen*

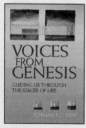

A brilliant blending of modern midrash and the life stages of Erik Erikson's developmental psychology. Shows how the pathways of our lives are quite similar to those of the leading figures of Genesis who speak directly to us, telling of their spiritual and emotional journeys.

6" x 9", 192 pp. HC, ISBN 1-879045-75-3 **$21.95**

ISRAEL—A SPIRITUAL TRAVEL GUIDE
A Companion for the Modern Jewish Pilgrim
by *Rabbi Lawrence A. Hoffman*

Be spiritually prepared for your journey to Israel.

A Jewish spiritual travel guide to Israel, helping today's pilgrim tap into the deep 249 spiritual meaning of the ancient—and modern—sites of the Holy Land. Combines in quick reference format ancient blessings, medieval prayers, biblical and historical references, and modern poetry. The only guidebook that helps readers to prepare spiritually for the occasion. More than a guide book: It is a spiritual map.

•AWARD WINNER•

Theology/Philosophy

•AWARD WINNER•

WINNER,
National Jewish
Book Award

A LIVING COVENANT
The Innovative Spirit in Traditional Judaism
by *David Hartman*

The Judaic tradition is often seen as being more concerned with uncritical obedience to law than with individual freedom and responsibility. Hartman challenges this approach by revealing a Judaism grounded in a covenant—a relational framework—informed by the metaphor of marital love rather than that of parent-child dependency.

"Jews and non-Jews, liberals and traditionalists will see classic Judaism anew in these pages."
—*Dr. Eugene B. Borowitz, Hebrew Union College–Jewish Institute of Religion*

6" x 9", 368 pp. Quality Paperback, ISBN 1-58023-011-3 **$18.95**

A HEART OF MANY ROOMS
Celebrating the Many Voices within Judaism
by *David Hartman*

With clarity, passion and outstanding scholarship, David Hartman addresses the spiritual and theological questions that face all Jews and all people today. From the perspective of traditional Judaism, he helps us understand the varieties of 20th-century Jewish practice and shows that commitment to both Jewish tradition and to pluralism can create bridges of understanding between people of different religious convictions.

"An extraordinary book, devoid of stereotypic thinking; lucid and pertinent, a modern classic."
—*Michael Walzer, Institute for Advanced Study, Princeton*

6" x 9", 352 pp. HC, ISBN 1-58023-048-2 **$24.95**

• CLASSICS BY ABRAHAM JOSHUA HESCHEL •

The Earth Is the Lord's: The Inner World of the Jew in Eastern Europe
5½" x 8", 112 pp, Quality Paperback, ISBN 1-879045-42-7 **$13.95**

Israel: An Echo of Eternity with new Introduction by Susannah Heschel
5½" x 8", 272 pp, Quality Paperback, ISBN 1-879045-70-2 **$18.95**

A Passion for Truth: Despair and Hope in Hasidism
5½" x 8", 352 pp, Quality Paperback, ISBN 1-879045-41-9 **$18.95**

• THEOLOGY & PHILOSOPHY...Other books•

Aspects of Rabbinic Theology by Solomon Schechter, with a new Introduction by Neil Gillman 6" x 9", 440 pp, Quality Paperback, ISBN 1-879045-24-9 **$18.95**

The Last Trial: On the Legends and Lore of the Command to Abraham to Offer Isaac as a Sacrifice by Shalom Spiegel, with a new Introduction by Judah Goldin
6" x 9", 208 pp, Quality Paperback, ISBN 1-879045-29-X **$17.95**

Judaism and Modern Man: An Interpretation of Jewish Religion by Will Herberg; new Introduction by Neil Gillman 5½" x 8½", 336 pp, Quality Paperback, ISBN 1-879045-87-7 **$18.95**

Seeking the Path to Life: Theological Meditations On God and the Nature of People, Love, Life and Death by Rabbi Ira F. Stone 6" x 9", 132 pp,
Quality Paperback, ISBN 1-879045-47-8 **$14.95**; HC, ISBN 1-879045-17-6 **$19.95**

The Spirit of Renewal: Finding Faith After the Holocaust by Edward Feld
6" x 9", 224 pp, Quality Paperback, ISBN 1-879045-40-0 **$16.95**

Tormented Master: The Life and Spiritual Quest of Rabbi Nahman of Bratslav
by Arthur Green 6" x 9", 408 pp, Quality Paperback, ISBN 1-879045-11-7 **$18.95**

Your Word Is Fire Ed. and trans. with a new Introduction by Arthur Green and Barry W. Holtz 6" x 9", 152 pp, Quality Paperback, ISBN 1-879045-25-7 **$14.95**

Art of Jewish Living Series for Holiday Observance

THE SHABBAT SEDER
by *Dr. Ron Wolfson*

A concise step by step guide designed to teach people the meaning and importance of this weekly celebration, as well as its practices.

Each chapter corresponds to one of ten steps that together comprise the Shabbat dinner ritual, and looks at the *concepts*, *objects*, and *meanings* behind the specific activity or ritual act. The blessings that accompany the meal are written in both Hebrew and English, and accompanied by English transliteration. Also included are craft projects, recipes, discussion ideas and other creative suggestions for enriching the Shabbat experience.

"A how-to book in the best sense...."
—*Dr. David Lieber, President, University of Judaism, Los Angeles*

7" x 9", 272 pp. Quality Paperback, ISBN 1-879045-90-7 **$16.95**

Also available are these helpful companions to *The Shabbat Seder*:
- •Booklet of the Blessings and Songs   ISBN 1-879045-91-5 $5.00
- •Audiocassette of the Blessings   DNO3 $6.00
- •Teacher's Guide   ISBN 1-879045-92-3 $4.95

HANUKKAH
by *Dr. Ron Wolfson*
Edited by *Joel Lurie Grishaver*

Designed to help celebrate and enrich the holiday season, *Hanukkah* discusses the holiday's origins, explores the reasons for the Hanukkah candles and customs, and provides everything from recipes to family activities.

There are songs, recipes, useful information on the arts and crafts of Hanukkah, the calendar and its relationship to Christmas time, and games played at Hanukkah. Putting the holiday in a larger, timely context, "December Dilemmas" deals with ways in which a Jewish family can cope with Christmas.

"Helpful for the family that strives to induct its members into the spirituality and joys of Jewishness and Judaism...a significant text in the neglected art of Jewish family education."
—*Rabbi Harold M. Schulweis, Cong. Valley Beth Shalom, Encino, CA*

7" x 9", 192 pp. Quality Paperback, ISBN 1-879045-97-4 **$16.95**

THE PASSOVER SEDER
by *Dr. Ron Wolfson*

Explains the concepts behind Passover ritual and ceremony in clear, easy-to-understand language, and offers step by step procedures for Passover observance and preparing the home for the holiday.

Easy to Follow Format: Using an innovative photo-documentary technique, real families describe in vivid images their own experiences with the Passover holiday. **Easy to Read Hebrew Texts:** The Haggadah texts in Hebrew, English, and transliteration are presented in a three-column format designed to help celebrants learn the meaning of the prayers and how to read them. **An Abundance of Useful Information:** A detailed description of how to perform the rituals is included, along with practical questions and answers, and imaginative ideas for Seder celebration.

"A creative 'how-to' for making the Seder a more meaningful experience."
—*Michael Strassfeld, co-author of* The Jewish Catalog

7" x 9", 336 pp. Quality Paperback, ISBN 1-879045-93-1 **$16.95**

Also available are these helpful companions to *The Passover Seder*:
- •Passover Workbook   ISBN 1-879045-94-X $6.95
- •Audiocassette of the Blessings   DNO4 $6.00
- •Teacher's Guide   ISBN 1-879045-95-8 $4.95

Healing/Recovery/Wellness

Experts Praise *Twelve Jewish Steps to Recovery*

"Recommended reading for people of all denominations."
—*Rabbi Abraham J. Twerski, M.D.*

TWELVE JEWISH STEPS TO RECOVERY
A Personal Guide to Turning from Alcoholism & Other Addictions...Drugs, Food, Gambling, Sex...
by *Rabbi Kerry M. Olitzky & Stuart A. Copans, M.D.*
Preface by *Abraham J. Twerski, M.D.*; Introduction by *Rabbi Sheldon Zimmerman*; "Getting Help" by *JACS Foundation*

A Jewish perspective on the Twelve Steps of addiction recovery programs with consolation, inspiration and motivation for recovery. It draws from traditional sources and quotes from what recovering Jewish people say about their experiences with addictions of all kinds. Inspiring illustrations of the twelve gates of the Old City of Jerusalem introduce each step.

6" x 9", 136 pp. Quality Paperback, ISBN 1-879045-09-5 **$13.95**

Recovery from Codependence: A Jewish Twelve Steps Guide to Healing Your Soul
by Rabbi Kerry M. Olitzky

6" x 9", 160 pp. Quality Paperback Original, ISBN 1-879045-32-X **$13.95**; HC, ISBN -27-3 **$21.95**

Renewed Each Day: Daily Twelve Step Recovery Meditations Based on the Bible
by Rabbi Kerry M. Olitzky & Aaron Z.

6" x 9", Quality Paperback Original, **V. I**, 224 pp. **$14.95**; **V. II**, 280 pp. **$16.95**

One Hundred Blessings Every Day: Daily Twelve Step Recovery Affirmations, Exercises for Personal Growth & Renewal Reflecting Seasons of the Jewish Year
by Rabbi Kerry M. Olitzky

4½" x 6½", 432 pp. Quality Paperback Original, ISBN 1-879045-30-3 **$14.95**

HEALING OF SOUL, HEALING OF BODY
Spiritual Leaders Unfold the Strength and Solace in Psalms
Edited by *Rabbi Simkha Y. Weintraub, CSW, for The Jewish Healing Center*

A source of solace for those who are facing illness, as well as those who care for them. The ten Psalms which form the core of this healing resource were originally selected 200 years ago by Rabbi Nachman of Breslov as a "complete remedy." Today, for anyone coping with illness, they continue to provide a wellspring of strength. Each Psalm is newly translated, making it clear and accessible, and each one is introduced by an eminent rabbi, men and women reflecting different movements and backgrounds. To all who are living with the pain and uncertainty of illness, this spiritual resource offers an anchor of spiritual comfort.

"Will bring comfort to anyone fortunate enough to read it. This gentle book is a luminous gem of wisdom."
—*Larry Dossey, M.D., author of* Healing Words: The Power of Prayer & the Practice of Medicine

6" x 9", 128 pp. Quality Paperback Original, illus., 2-color text, ISBN 1-879045-31-1 **$14.95**

Life Cycle

GRIEF IN OUR SEASONS
A Mourner's Kaddish Companion
by *Rabbi Kerry M. Olitzky*

Strength from the Jewish tradition for the first year of mourning.

Provides a wise and inspiring selection of sacred Jewish writings and a simple, powerful ancient ritual for mourners to read each day, to help hold the memory of their loved ones in their hearts. It offers a comforting, step by step daily link to saying *Kaddish*.

"A hopeful, compassionate guide along the journey from grief to rebirth from mourning to a new morning."
—*Rabbi Levi Meier, Ph.D., Chaplain, Cedars–Sinai Medical Center, Los Angeles*

4½" x 6½", 448 pp. Quality Paperback Original, ISBN 1-879045-55-9 **$15.95**

MOURNING & MITZVAH
• WITH OVER 60 GUIDED EXERCISES •
A Guided Journal for Walking the Mourner's Path Through Grief to Healing
by *Anne Brener, L.C.S.W.*; Foreword by *Rabbi Jack Riemer*; Introduction by *Rabbi William Cutter*

"Fully engaging in mourning means you will be a different person than before you began." **For those who mourn a death, for those who would help them,** for those who face a loss of any kind, Brener teaches us the power and strength available to us in the fully experienced mourning process. Guided writing exercises help stimulate the processes of both conscious and unconscious healing.

"A stunning book! It offers an exploration in depth of the place where psychology and religious ritual intersect, and the name of that place is Truth."
—*Rabbi Harold Kushner, author of* When Bad Things Happen to Good People

7½" x 9", 288 pp. Quality Paperback Original, ISBN 1-879045-23-0 **$19.95**

A TIME TO MOURN, A TIME TO COMFORT
A Guide to Jewish Bereavement and Comfort
by *Dr. Ron Wolfson*

A guide to meeting the needs of those who mourn and those who seek to provide comfort in times of sadness. While this book is written from a layperson's point of view, it also includes the specifics for funeral preparations and practical guidance for preparing the home and family to sit *shiva*.

"A sensitive and perceptive guide to Jewish tradition. Both those who mourn and those who comfort will find it a map to accompany them through the whirlwind."
—*Deborah E. Lipstadt, Emory University*

7" x 9", 336 pp. Quality Paperback, ISBN 1-879045-96-6 **$16.95**

WHEN A GRANDPARENT DIES
A Kid's Own Remembering Workbook for Dealing with Shiva and the Year Beyond
by *Nechama Liss-Levinson, Ph.D.*

Drawing insights from both psychology and Jewish tradition, this workbook helps children participate in the process of mourning, offering guided exercises, rituals, and places to write, draw, list, create and express their feelings.

"Will bring support, guidance, and understanding for countless children, teachers, and health professionals."
—*Rabbi Earl A. Grollman, D.D., author of* Talking about Death

8" x 10", 48 pp. HC, illus., 2-color text, ISBN 1-879045-44-3 **$15.95**

Life Cycle

A HEART OF WISDOM
Making the Jewish Journey from Midlife Through the Elder Years
Edited by *Susan Berrin*

We are all growing older. *A Heart of Wisdom* shows us how to understand our own process of aging—and the aging of those we care about—from a Jewish perspective, from midlife through the elder years.

How does Jewish tradition influence our own aging? How does living, thinking and worshipping as a Jew affect us as we age? How can Jewish tradition help us retain our dignity as we age? Offers insights and enlightenment from Jewish tradition.

6" x 9", 384 pp. Quality Paperback, ISBN 1-58023-051-2 **$18.95**; HC, ISBN 1-879045-73-7 **$24.95**

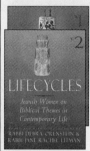

LIFECYCLES
V. 1: Jewish Women on Life Passages & Personal Milestones
Edited and with Introductions by *Rabbi Debra Orenstein*
V. 2: Jewish Women on Biblical Themes in Contemporary Life
Edited and with Introductions by
Rabbi Debra Orenstein and *Rabbi Jane Rachel Litman*

This unique multivolume collaboration brings together over one hundred women writers, rabbis, and scholars to create the first comprehensive work on Jewish life cycle that fully includes women's perspectives.

•Award Winner•

V. 1: 6" x 9", 480 pp. Quality Paperback, ISBN 1-58023-018-0 **$19.95**
HC, ISBN 1-879045-14-1 **$24.95**

V. 2: 6" x 9", 464 pp. Quality Paperback, ISBN 1-58023-019-9 **$19.95**
HC, ISBN 1-879045-15-X **$24.95**

Life Cycle— The Art of Jewish Living Series for Holiday Observance
by Dr. Ron Wolfson

Hanukkah—7" x 9", 192 pp. Quality Paperback, ISBN 1-879045-97-4 **$16.95**

The Shabbat Seder—7" x 9", 272 pp. Quality Paperback, ISBN 1-879045-90-7 **$16.95**; Booklet of Blessings **$5.00**; Audiocassette of Blessings **$6.00**; Teacher's Guide **$4.95**

The Passover Seder—7" x 9", 336 pp. Quality Paperback, ISBN 1-879045-93-1 **$16.95**; Passover Workbook, **$6.95**; Audiocassette of Blessings, **$6.00**; Teacher's Guide, **$4.95**

• Life Cycle...Other Books •

Bar/Bat Mitzvah Basics: A Practical Family Guide to Coming of Age Together
Ed. by Cantor Helen Leneman 6" x 9", 240 pp. Quality Paperback, ISBN 1-879045-54-0 **$16.95**

Embracing the Covenant: Converts to Judaism Talk About Why & How
Ed. and with Intros. by Rabbi Allan L. Berkowitz and Patti Moskovitz
6" x 9", 192 pp. Quality Paperback, ISBN 1-879045-50-8 **$15.95**

For Kids—Putting God on Your Guest List: How to Claim the Spiritual Meaning of Your Bar or Bat Mitzvah by Rabbi Jeffrey K. Salkin
6" x 9", 144 pp. Quality Paperback Original, ISBN 1-58023-015-6 **$14.95**

The New Jewish Baby Book: Names, Ceremonies, Customs—A Guide for Today's Families by Anita Diamant 6" x 9", 336 pp. Quality Paperback, ISBN 1-879045-28-1 **$16.95**

Putting God on the Guest List, 2nd Ed.: How to Reclaim the Spiritual Meaning of Your Child's Bar or Bat Mitzvah by Rabbi Jeffrey K. Salkin
6" x 9", 224 pp. Quality Paperback, ISBN 1-897045-59-1 **$16.95**; HC, ISBN 1-879045-58-3 **$24.95**

Tears of Sorrow, Seeds of Hope: A Jewish Spiritual Companion for Infertility and Pregnancy Loss by Rabbi Nina Beth Cardin
6" x 9", 192 pp. HC, ISBN 1-58023-017-2 **$19.95**

So That Your Values Live On: Ethical Wills & How to Prepare Them
Ed. by Rabbi Jack Riemer & Professor Nathaniel Stampfer
6" x 9", 272 pp. Quality Paperback, ISBN 1-879045-34-6 **$17.95**

Children's Spirituality

For ages 8 and up

BUT GOD REMEMBERED
Stories of Women from Creation to the Promised Land
by *Sandy Eisenberg Sasso*, Full-color illus. by *Bethanne Andersen*

NONDENOMINATIONAL, NONSECTARIAN

A fascinating collection of four different stories of women only briefly mentioned in biblical tradition and religious texts, but never before explored. Award-winning author Sasso brings to life the intriguing stories of Lilith, Serach, Bityah, and the Daughters of Z, courageous and strong women from ancient tradition. All teach important values through their faith and actions.

9" x 12", 32 pp. HC, Full-color illus., ISBN 1-879045-43-5 **$16.95**

•AWARD WINNER•

IN GOD'S NAME
For ages 4 and up

by *Sandy Eisenberg Sasso*
Full-color illustrations by *Phoebe Stone*

Selected by Parent Council, Ltd.™

MULTICULTURAL, NONDENOMINATIONAL, NONSECTARIAN

Like an ancient myth in its poetic text and vibrant illustrations, this modern fable about the search for God's name celebrates the diversity and, at the same time, the unity of all the people of the world. Each seeker claims he or she alone knows the answer. Finally, they come together and learn what God's name really is, sharing the ultimate harmony of belief in one God by people of all faiths, all backgrounds.

•AWARD WINNER•

9" x 12", 32 pp. HC, Full color illus., ISBN 1-879045-26-5 **$16.95**

For ages 4 and up

GOD IN BETWEEN

by *Sandy Eisenberg Sasso*
Full-color illustrations by *Sally Sweetland*

NONDENOMINATIONAL, NONSECTARIAN, MULTICULTURAL

If you wanted to find God, where would you look?

A magical, mythical tale that teaches that God can be found where we are: within all of us and the relationships between us.

9" x 12", 32 pp. HC, Full-color illus., ISBN 1-879045-86-9 **$16.95**

IN OUR IMAGE
God's First Creatures
For ages 4 and up

by *Nancy Sohn Swartz*, Full-color illustrations by *Melanie Hall*

NONDENOMINATIONAL, NONSECTARIAN

A playful new twist to the Creation story. Celebrates the interconnectedness of nature and the harmony of all living things.

9" x 12", 32 pp. HC, Full-color illus., ISBN 1-879045-99-0 **$16.95**

•AWARD WINNER•

For ages 4 and up

GOD'S PAINTBRUSH

by *Sandy Eisenberg Sasso*
Full-color illustrations by *Annette Compton*

MULTICULTURAL, NONDENOMINATIONAL, NONSECTARIAN

Invites children of all faiths and backgrounds to encounter God openly in their own lives. Wonderfully interactive, provides questions adult and child can explore together at the end of each episode.

11" x 8½", 32 pp. HC, Full-color illus., ISBN 1-879045-22-2 **$16.95**

***Also Available!* Teacher's Guide: A Guide for Jewish & Christian Educators and Parents**

8½" x 11", 32 pp. PB, ISBN 1-879045-57-5 **$6.95**

Children's Spirituality

A PRAYER FOR THE EARTH
The Story of Naamah, Noah's Wife

For ages 4 and up

by *Sandy Eisenberg Sasso*
Full-color illustrations by *Bethanne Andersen*

NONDENOMINATIONAL, NONSECTARIAN

This new story, based on an ancient text, opens readers' religious imaginations to new ideas about the well-known story of the Flood. When God tells Noah to bring the animals of the world onto the ark, God *also* calls on Naamah, Noah's wife, to save each plant on Earth.

> "A lovely tale....Children of all ages should be drawn to this parable for our times."
>
> —*Tomie dePaola, artist/author of books for children*

•AWARD WINNER•

9" x 12", 32 pp. HC, Full-color illus., ISBN 1-879045-60-5 **$16.95**

THE 11TH COMMANDMENT
Wisdom from Our Children

For all ages

by The Children of America

MULTICULTURAL, NONDENOMINATIONAL, NONSECTARIAN

"If there were an Eleventh Commandment, what would it be?"

Children of many religious denominations across America answer this question—in their own drawings and words—in *The 11th Commandment.*

> "Wonderful....This unusual book provides both food for thought and insight into the hopes and fears of today's young."
>
> —*American Library Association's* Booklist

8" x 10", 48 pp. HC, Full-color illus., ISBN 1-879045-46-X **$16.95**

SHARING BLESSINGS
Children's Stories for Exploring the Spirit of the Jewish Holidays

For ages 6 and up

by *Rahel Musleah* and *Rabbi Michael Klayman*
Full-color illustrations by *Mary O'Keefe Young*

What is the spiritual message of each of the Jewish holidays?
How do we teach it to our children?

Many books tell children about the historical significance and customs of the holidays. Now, through engaging, creative stories about one family's spiritual preparation, *Sharing Blessings* explores ways to get into the *spirit* of 13 different holidays.

> "A beguiling introduction to important Jewish values by way of the holidays."
>
> —*Rabbi Harold Kushner, author of* When Bad Things Happen
> to Good People *and* How Good Do We Have to Be?

7" x 10", 64 pp. HC, Full-color illus., ISBN 1-879045-71-0 **$18.95**

THE BOOK OF MIRACLES
For ages 9–13
A Young Person's Guide to Jewish Spiritual Awareness

by *Lawrence Kushner*

With a Special 10th Anniversary Introduction and all new illustrations by the author.

From the miracle at the Red Sea to the miracle of waking up this morning, this intriguing book introduces kids to a way of everyday spiritual thinking to last a lifetime. Kushner, whose award-winning books have brought spirituality to life for countless adults, now shows young people how to use Judaism as a foundation on which to build their lives.

6" x 9", 96 pp. HC, 2-color illus., ISBN 1-879045-78-8 **$16.95**